369

STORIES
YOUR PATH OF ENLIGHTENMENT
ONE STORY AT A TIME

369

STORIES
YOUR PATH OF ENLIGHTENMENT
ONE STORY AT A TIME

Binais Begovic

Eigengro Publishing
2019

First Printing: 2019

ISBN 978-1-7332321-1-1

Eigengro Publishing
www.eigengro.com
info@eigengro.com

Ordering Information:
Quantity sales. Special discounts are available on quantity purchases by corporations, associations, and others. For details, contact the "Special Sales Department" at the address above.

Dedication to my loves Cat & Layla

Dear Cat & Layla,

Without you two, this book wouldn't be possible.
Without your love for me, I wouldn't be possible.
My thoughts and words have taken me to some
incredible places, but I'm still struggling to find
words that can describe my gratitude and love for
the both of you and what you mean to me. I will just
leave it here and I will let my actions hold me
accountable as I dedicate the rest of my life
to love you two the best way I can.

Eternal Love,
Binais

Contents

#Story60: Question: What would you tell someone that hates herself?

#Story61: Creativity.

#Story62: L E A - Love - Expression – Attention

#Story63: Indoctrination.

#Story64: Question: How to step out of your comfort zone?

#Story65: Don't train your mind. It's not your pet.

#Story66: Can a person change you?

#Story67: Why do we sometimes feel discontent with ourselves?

#Story68: Emotional deformities.

#Story69: Networking or flex of egos?

#Story70: What books are the right books?

#Story71: Question: How to deal with the fear of losing
someone you love?

#Story72: Fear of failure. Pressure.

#Story73: You can't offend me with judgments.

#Story74: What Is EXISTENCE?

#Story75: De-Press-Ion.

#Story76: Is ignorance bliss?

#Story77: En(LIE)ghtenment

#Story78: Mommy & Daddy issues.

#Story79: Women with Daddy issues.

#Story80: Men with Daddy issues.

#Story81: Life can only be experienced.

#Story82: Sacrifice is success, not sacrifice.

#Story83: So why do we have prisons if what people did
in the past doesn't matter?

#Story84: Letting go of the past.

#Story85: Letting go vs. forgiveness.

#Story86: Humanity against issues, not humanity against people.

#Story87: Parenting through guidance.

*"My struggles and darkness
were once my only friends.
When I fully embraced them,
they showed me beauty in life
I never knew existed."*

—Binais

An Intimate Reflection

From Ashes with Love

As I am entering 2019, sitting with my precious wife and my daughter around our beautiful fire pit at home, I am trying to express my journey through words. Words are powerful, after all. God is a word. Love is a word. Life is a word. We create and we destroy through words, so I take words somewhat seriously nowadays. I'm reflecting back on the year that has past; a year that has changed my life forever; a year that has changed everything inside and around me. A year ago, on this day around the same time I was in the middle of a fire, an inferno; a fire that was nothing compared to what this fire is today.

I was a different man. I was in between being broken and being glued together. I say glued because I've always had an ability to keep it all together and find a way to present it all in the best possible package. But last year, it was different. It was like nothing I've ever experienced before. It was stronger. It was deeper. Perhaps my awareness had slowly started sneaking up on me as I was midway through a journey of my lifetime. A journey of discovering it all - all the broken pieces, what they are, and what type of glue was holding it together. I was at a point of having it and knowing it all, but yet, I had nothing and I didn't know anything. Some people call it Enlightenment.

About To Face It All

The most precious people and things I had in my life I couldn't even access, see, feel, or find a way to enrich their lives with my presence. All the things I had surrounded myself with were a part of my life puzzle. When all the pieces were put together, they projected a nice picture of having it all. I displayed it so strangers could admire it in an attempt to find joy and happiness through them that I couldn't feel myself.

Why was their validation so essential for my existence? What was going on? Who was I? What was I? Why was I unable to feel any substance or fulfillment? Why wasn't I able to just be present, without feeling a constant pull from something, somewhere? I always had to be somewhere, do something, fix something, create something, and yet I was nowhere and did nothing. My life was on repeat. Was this all just a simulation of life? Was this a nightmare or my reality? Was my life even real? Were my friends real? What was real and what wasn't? Why was everyone telling me how lucky I was, yet I felt like a miserable mess living on high octane fuel, thriving on the heroic egoistic projection of life?

I was about to face it all. I was about to find out. And whatever discovery I was about to make, I would have to accept it. I was about to face something that most of us fear but we don't know why. I was about
to find the truth-my truth in its rawest form - darkness in its own spotlight. I was about to stand naked, stripped of everything I once thought was important. I realized it was the only way for me to find what I somehow knew must exist. I was about to let it all go. I was about to let go of a life that I did (not) choose to live and let go of a person that I did (not) choose to become. I was about to face reality and my own truth. The product of that journey is this book and everything I've discovered through an intense year of searching for everything that my intuition was whispering to me about.

We Are Going To Be Ok

This book is my gift to you as a thank you for helping me find some of the answers. But it's mainly a gift to myself and my family, as I need a proper guide that makes sense to me and a reminder of what is important as I go about life, just in case I ever forget what life is truly about.

"369 Stories" is a brief summary of my year long journey and the discoveries I've made through an intensified search "for more" in life. It's the journey of my personal "rebirth"; a complete transformation of consciousness by dissolving everything that wasn't me and by rebuilding from scratch, while learning to live and love from ashes. This is my way of reaching out to other souls out there to let you know that we are going to be okay. We just got distracted and forgot where to look along this eternal journey called life. I have no expectations, but I do hope that this book can help you. If it helps one person, I would consider it to be a success.

Enlightenment

Some may associate enlightenment with the key to success and knowledge that will sweep everyone off their feet. A shortcut to gain power, to be remembered, to go on a mountain top for a few years, escaping it all in search for wisdom and meaning of life. For me and my personal journey, it has been about finding answers so I could save my marriage, be a good father to my daughter, understand her and what really makes her happy, and not what I think makes her happy. Being able to spend time with my wife without being attacked by thoughts, pressure, guilt, or distraction. Being able to understand where all the temptation is coming from and why I have no ability to fight it, no matter how hard I try.

Enlightenment for me has been about helping my wife find her truths and helping her heal from her wounds by guiding her into recognizing where it all comes from, while at the same time finding new ways to eliminate possible fights and battles from the same things that held our lives in a chokehold.

Enlightenment to me has been a journey of self-discovery that led me to answers and understanding about unconditional love. Enlightenment for me has been about waking up in the morning and instead of checking my phone, I look over and watch my beautiful wife and daughter sleeping peacefully, doing nothing else but just look at them while being filled with immense love and light. Enlightenment for me has been about finding a way to tell my friends and family that I no longer can be the person who can meet their expectations. It has been about me not feeling fear of pointing out the obvious faults in judgments disguised as compliments during some of the most amazing dinners with former business and personal friends.

Enlightenment for me has been about me finding answers to why I feel pressure to speak in a certain way, to dress a certain way, to title myself, and to belong to something or someone for the sake of an image I'm trying to uphold. Enlightenment for me has been about finding beauty in people's souls that are not related to what they own, what they wear, how they look like, and how they present themselves. Enlightenment for me has been about enjoying sitting in a chair all alone for hours and traveling in my thoughts to places I didn't even know existed because they were blocked by social constructs and programs. Enlightenment for me has been about helping others light their candle with my own candle while realizing that my candle would still burn bright. Enlightenment has been about removing layer after layer of emotional wounds, triggers, pain, suffering, and false knowledge that I had been guarding for unknown reasons. Enlightenment for me has been about finding God on my own terms while looking for answers and asking for help and guidance to show me how to love my life, my family, my neighbors, my followers, animals, and my planet. Enlightenment for me has been about finding truth in lies and finding lies in truth. Enlightenment for me has been me finding strength while standing stripped down to my bare soul being judged, hated, observed, and questioned. It has been about finding strength in my lowest points in my life, while asking if there were any point continuing. Enlightenment for me was finding light and answers in those moments of darkness when there was no hope and I was about to count my last minutes on earth. Enlightenment for me has been about finding balance and happiness in simply existing and embracing everything as is.

"Enlightenment is not about power. It's about finding love, peace, and harmony in life. Ego seeks knowledge. Soul seeks answers. They both need to be balanced and in harmony. Nobody can give you enlightenment. It's your personal choices you make in life that can either bring you closer to your higher self or take you further away from your truth. Your ability to be vulnerable plays a big part. If we constantly keep our guard up, we can never make room for light and love to come in. Vulnerability, search for answers, and your ability to monitor your inner peace can all help you on your path to enlightenment."

#Story1: Ask me a question.

I never searched for Enlightenment. I just searched for happiness. I searched for the ability to love those who loved me. I didn't know that the search would lead to Enlightenment. It was a terrifying lightning strike that came suddenly one night, a little over a year ago. An event that would change my life forever. I quickly realized that Enlightenment would be a destructive force if I did not heal my personal wounds. I didn't know where to start the search or how to find what needed to be healed, but my awareness would not let me fool myself. It would not let me get away with anything. My awareness was going after my own ass, and it forced me into isolation and into cleaning up my own mess, mixed with generation after generation of inherited wounds, programs, traumas, judgmental views and opinions, social norms, pressure, and paradigms. That's what this journey is about. The 369 stories in this book are a part of that healing journey.

The journey started on my Instagram stories through Q&A's. One day I woke up and something in me made me post an IG story "Ask Me a Question." I was shaking, sweating, and my heart was pounding hard. It was anxiety and fear and I had never had anxiety before. I feared what I was about to discover. I knew that I no longer was able to lie to myself and every question that I answered would be as honest as

I possibly could be. I was not going to show myself any mercy. I decided to strip down to my bare soul by putting myself out there to be asked, questioned, judged, tested, observed, attacked, but also loved, triggered, cheered for, and supported by so many wonderful souls. Each day was a new story and a new battle I had to fight. Each day was a new discovery. The growth was painful and silent, but the victories were rewarding and loud.

369 Stories are a part of that journey and a part of my discoveries during my "pilgrim year." It's a combination of my personal confessions, raw conversations with my followers, their stories that were inspired by my stories, my discoveries of everything helpful that I could find within the indoctrination and within the esoteric side of knowledge that could help me find any answers that would let my fear and pain disappear. Every story is unrelated, but connected. Regardless of how you read this book or what story you start with first, you will be able to follow that journey. Each story is related to specific discoveries and events, but there is no particular order. Buckle up for an exciting ride.

#Story2: Everything is nothing. Nothing is everything.

Once I had reached a point in my life when I had "everything" that most people in this world would consider as the "ultimate success" - living my dream in LA, having an amazing and loving family, living in the home I had always wanted, dream cars, even feeling healthy and strong, a family that loved me beyond everything - it wasn't enough.

"Maybe I need more of all of this - bigger house, more cars, a plane perhaps, maybe my family needs to love me better and different," I thought to myself. Suddenly, one evening, I experienced a flash of light, a vision. It gave me the strength to ask myself why I felt like I had nothing. I saw my family smile, but I couldn't feel their joy or happiness. It was like I was observing my life, but I had no access to it. I belonged to something else and that thing didn't care about me. It was a moment that changed everything. I decided to try to see what is actually real and what is false in this world. Layer by layer, as I was releasing myself from all debaucheries and lies, I became filled with more light and more ability to see my personal world, and the world in general, with fresh eyes. Parts of that journey I now choose to share with some of you. A part of that journey is also me finally finding my purpose that is now slowly manifesting itself into different creations and seeds that I've planted as I've finally started living my life without a blindfold.

#Story3: Purpose, curse, or a gift?

It's been an intense week of discoveries as I'm searching for deeper answers and understanding the pain and suffering among people from all walks of life. Pressure, responsibilities, guilt, expectations, heartbreaks, blame, anger, frustration, depression, suicide, burnout, despair, misunderstandings, loneliness, and isolation are just some of our human by products that have heavily infested themselves in our society. I have to dig deep for some of the answers and truthfully, it gets exhausting. Not because of how I search but because of what I have seen when I search. People are aware of all the problems, but most are completely unaware of their causes.

The misconception about causes, rapid transmutation of all the mentioned issues, absence of awareness and limited solutions that are currently being offered are truly concerning. As I search and discover all of this while trying to help those affected who search themselves to me, I instantly make myself responsible for being the one who fearlessly has to face all of it while feeling everyone's pain as I need to stay strong for them.

As I'm writing this, I wonder if it's a gift or a curse. Maybe it's both? Maybe it's my purpose and my calling? Who can give me answers if I can't do it myself, (the guy who always thinks he knows it all)? I have also realized this is no longer about me. This is about everyone.

This is also the first time in my life that I can't identify anyone or anything to blame for what we have become. It's all of us together, but nobody wants to take responsibility for anything. Where do I start? How do I start? Why do I start? I have answers to many of my questions as I now search for ways to discredit my own answers...

#Story4: We are not alone.

There were times in life when I felt like I was sinking and being sucked into this black hole. For no particular reason, even when things seemed to be in perfect harmony seen from the outside. Each time this occurred, I somehow found my way out. I started instantly focusing on five reasons why my life is important and significant. Each time, I discovered new reasons presented as a disguise.

It's interesting that I couldn't see those reasons while I was being overwhelmed by everyday noise. Was the black hole I was sinking into a safe place? A reminder? The times I felt alone and like nobody cared, despite being surrounded by people that loved and cared about me, it seemed that my desperate scream for help wasn't loud enough. Perhaps my cries were blocked by my invisible enemies - anger, frustration, and resentment - while pushing everyone away from me. How could they know anything, when I barely knew what was going on? Does life really have to be like this? Why wasn't I able to recognize the true enemies in this case? It wasn't people that I tried to push away, it was my invisible enemies that I somehow recognized as guards.

Now as I am sitting here and writing this, I start to wonder how many people have tried to scream for help right in front of my eyes without my ability to see or hear them due to my own walls and blocks combined with theirs. Could I have saved someone? I'm sorry everyone if I haven't heard you before. I've come a long way. I'm here now. I'm going to be okay. You're going to be okay too. We get pushed into black holes of infinite despair, but there are ways out. There are many ways out.

"There were times in life when
I felt like I was sinking and
being sucked into this black hole.
For no particular reason,
even when things seemed
to be in perfect harmony
seen from the outside."

#Story5: The Law of (dis)obedience.

There are two sides of us. One that obeys and follows social conditioning, patriarchal and matriarchal programming, religion, authority, educational programs, teachers, employers. The same side follows and idolizes "human gods," celebrities, fashion trends, falls for peer pressure, and marketing tricks. This is the Obedience program and it is the foundation of the entire society that is imprinted on us as soon as we open our eyes on Earth by our parents or guardians.

Now the beauty of the free will that was given to us is the opposing balancing imprint that I've identified as Disobedience or the Rebellion ego. It's the part of us that questions everything and everyone, that secretly has a separate agenda from the one that we present to the public. The Rebellion Disobedience program is the one that doesn't allow humanity to turn us into human robots, artificial intelligence. The Disobedience Rebellion Ego is the curious rebel that always searches for "more." The issue is when the conflict between Obedience and Disobedience in us becomes so disruptive that it blurs our vision and stops us from functioning the way society and the system expects us to in everyday life. Not understanding or embracing the dualistic conflict of the human mind can be the root of mental imbalances.

The goal is to be at peace with both. It's the only way to achieve internal and external peace and harmony. Until then, it will always seem to be chaos, when in fact, there is a perfect order at all the times. The chaos is in our head. This is when we become vulnerable and open to being snatched and serving different agendas in society, such as politics, big corporations' marketing tricks, trends, wars, and conflicts. Peace in the world starts the moment you are at a complete peace with your Obedience and Disobedience programs. Peace starts when they live and exist in perfect harmony. It's a journey of many miles to get there but so worth it.

#Story6: Friendship.

Obligations, agendas, expectations, burden, and pressure. For almost a year, I tried to free myself and others around me from those attachments when it comes to friendships. To compensate for the above, I added a touch of honesty and a dose or two of communication. A lot has happened. Some people left, some came, and some never left my side no matter what. I think it worked well. I feel free and I feel that others can feel free to be themselves around me. Trust will handle the rest from there. It will grow on its own with full transparency and without fear.

At this point, I'm ready to compromise. I'm okay to turn it into semi-conditional relationships and follow up on a few mutually agreed upon obligations. As long as everything comes from a place of good intent, purity, and it serves everyone's well-being, I truly am open to compromise.

#Story7: The world against me or me against the world?

As within, so without. It was one of those gloomy mornings where everything and everyone seemed to be against me again. Days like this are tough. But it is truly all in my head. I've seen this pattern so many times. Today, I decided to play a trick on my mind. I decided to call everyone "my friend" no matter how they treated me as far it was within socially acceptable conversation. By lunchtime, the thing - the feeling of the world being against me - released me. I suddenly started seeing and feeling love from everyone. It was just simply magical. Wait, just like that? I got the whole world to love me? But how? Aha, a mind trick again. But this time around, the joke is on you, dear mind. How does that feel? Try to pull that one on me ever again and I'll show you more tricks than David Copperfield in his prime.

#Story8: Being (Sm)art.

I recently discovered that the way I speak to you through these words and the way we connect to each other with each story is the same way that art has been speaking and connecting for thousands of years. There has always been a clear message, but somehow up until now, art was a foreign language to me. Now, when I view art, it somehow takes me to some wonderful places and realizations. When opinions and expressions were silenced so many times throughout history, we were allowed to paint, draw, and sculpt. Through art, we have channeled our thoughts, emotions, pain, and joy; it's truly magical that art is such a powerful language. Maybe I'll finally have a conversation with Mona Lisa one of these days and see what she tells me. It turns out that DaVinci was ahead of his time for real. He spoke about time travel and he wasn't lying. He just never told us how, but I get it now.

I've simply come to the realization that art is such a powerful and true way that people express themselves. Those feelings they were projecting through their painting, drawing, or sculpture were so real that they actually time traveled. Maybe it was their scream for help, maybe it was their way of saying humanity needs to change, or maybe they were simply just speaking to one specific person. Either way, the message was so powerful that it spoke for all of us. That's why we find a piece powerful, mysterious and fascinating. Those feelings are universal. Love, trust, betrayal, anger, happiness, sorrow, hope...we are all that artist.

The same goes for music. Do you think it's an accident that we love certain songs, artists, or albums and there is this specific song or artist that we can listen to over and over again at a certain stage of our life, but then later in life, we still may like the song, but it doesn't have the same meaning anymore? That's because our emotions have evolved or we have grown as people. Music and art are never truly just music and art. They help us trigger and decode our own thoughts, emotions, wounds, dreams. Art has no limits, no rules, it's infinite.

#Story9: Can't automate wisdom. Living a Lie. Selling lies.

Those who live in a lie, may only know lies. Those who live in a lie, will try to sell you a lie. Perfectly packaged, presented, automated, and served to you as the ultimate solution to all your life's problems. Every Era has known them, every civilization has faced them. You will recognize them easily. They bend for the truth. They run away from the truth. They get angry and defensive when faced by truth. Their magic tricks become visible, once you peek your head behind the curtain of that stage of theirs. Don't be surprised if they defend their lies, as lies are the only truth they know. Don't expect an apology or a change in behavior from them. You're in charge of it all. You're always in charge of what you make relevant and real in your life.

*"You're always in charge
of what you make relevant
and real in your life."*

#Story10: Selfish selfless act of selfcare.

It's not about focusing on ourselves. It's about taking a moment to reflect and ask ourselves - what the heck are we even doing? Where are we going? Why are we doing what we are doing? Does it serve us and our truth at all or do we belong to some program and agenda that we don't even know about? What would happen if we don't continue with what we are doing? Would our life be over? If so, then we are not free, we belong to something that can take our life anytime...

#Story11: We don't belong to our pasts or our past choices.

Today I learned to not let my past put duct tape over my mouth and a blindfold on my eyes. Only because my previous path in life, on the surface, was something that I criticize or disagree with today, this doesn't take away my freedom to speak. I no longer belong to my past or my choices. I now belong to the truth and my current intentions. My motivation to seek, speak, create, contribute, change, and help comes from all the right intentions. My past lost its battle against my present once I discovered how powerful the here and now is. The only purpose my past still serves is the filter for those who choose to judge me based on who I once was.

"My past lost its battle against my present once I discovered how powerful the here and now is."

#Story12: My balance is my main compass.

I'm truly starting to see the world more vibrantly than before. My days have become more peaceful since I stopped searching for harmony in the physical realm. It's a three-dimensional projection of our inner well-being, so I might as well project my own inner balance and peace, while I walk throughout the day. It's the main compass I can trust after all. But if the world still triggers me, I don't mind. How else will I be able to find what needs to be healed?

#Story13: Rebellious Millennials.

No, millennials are not lazy. They are just correcting the byproducts of previous generations' accomplishments. It's thanks to Millennials and their Disobedient Rebellious spirit that we have social media. Thanks to Millennials, we are now able to bypass all major master programs, including the filters of traditional media, and speak directly to each other as we have never had before.

The new generation has completely rejected what previous generations believed were life essentials such as working in cubicles, large diamond engagement rings, ideologies, dogmas, and homes and family before the age of 30. While previous generations were building and chasing materialistic fulfillment, their kids unfortunately got less attention and many felt lonely. Therefore, many of them rejected the things that their parents were chasing.

Thus, was the growth of social media. Now love, likes, and hearts are pouring in from strangers. I'm so proud of the new generation for not giving up and for getting creative when it came to searching for love through validation and instant gratification. Social media filled the void. But there's still a lot of good from previous generations - the key is to find a balance between the old and the new.

#Story14: Lust live love lie.

I found a way of beating LUST without suppressing my sexual energy. It was one of the biggest victories of my life and the most beautiful feeling I have ever experienced. The moment the lust grip let go of me, it opened up a whole new world and elevated my awareness to new heights. My IG feed filled with half-naked girls, my browser with bookmarked porn pages, all the sex fantasies suddenly became irrelevant. It was liberating.

Greed was right there next to it, but lust, that monster is something else...I won't be missing you, that's for sure.

"It was one of the biggest victories of my life and the most beautiful feeling I have ever experienced. The moment the lust grip let go of me."

#Story15: I got you, my old new dear friend.

(A message correspondence to a friend)

Going through the motions of life to attain those goals you've been chasing can help you tap into a variety of vibratory fields that carry messages related to human kind. It's an accelerated version of personal growth that most people never experience. Love to and from your family helped you heal. Your awareness has been raised to levels that surpasses most. Currently, you're in a dimension where you can see enough in order to understand that there is so much more, but not enough to keep your thoughts grounded. You, my friend, are approaching a heavy phase where you'll need to fight an extremely important fight. You'll have many more after that one, but you'll only start noticing them after you win this one. I'm talking about lust. For your level of consciousness, it will not be enough to restrain it. You will need to bring it close, face it, channel, develop and sublimate it until it completely releases you. The release will open up a new world for you where your new life starts. The new clarity will make you see the entire world with fresh eyes and everything you have known so far and believed in, you will discover is incomplete.

The love for your family and their love for you will be the ultimate truth that will help you make all the right choices. I say right because I can't help people whose intentions are not aligned with mine. However,

I've decided to believe in you and your intentions. If those intentions at any time change, I'll be gone from your life without any explanation and I'm afraid you'll have to continue on your own.

I'm not a teacher, I'm a guide. I'll never be able to teach you anything without you giving me a chance to walk you through scenarios of life so you can see everything for yourself. From there, you'll need to make all your own choices. Those choices can't be controlled or manipulated by me because I would be living against my own truth and against your truth as well.

"I'm not a teacher, I'm a guide. I'll never be able to teach you anything without you giving me a chance to walk you through scenarios of life so you can see everything for yourself."

#Story16: To my dear daughter Layla.

I just want to tell you that you are perfect and complete just the way you are. No title, no definition, no pressure needed. Everything you discover and experience in your lifejourney are just choices based on your personal truth. I want to remove any pressure from you that you have to be a certain way so you can spread your wings and fly above it all and land wherever you think is your true landing place, full of joy and light.

#Story17: What am I to you?

I hope to be your mirror of self-reflection, so you are able to see what you need to adjust in your own journey without my direct input and advice. Everyone's journey is different and circumstances are unpredictable variables. I know that we have never met, but somehow, I feel that I've known you for quite some time.

#Story18: Escape vs Growth:

Escape = Looking for solutions to your problems on the surface and the outside world.
Growth = Looking inwards within yourself.
Escape = Running away from yourself.
Growth = Face to face with yourself and your demons.

#Story19: Nothing to hide, everything to cry.

It's very hard to open up as a man. The fear of being judged and seen as weak is real. This compartmentalization has been going on for way too long. It's time for us to slowly evolve into multidimensional mental, spiritual and emotional beings. Let's start by never judging men for who we are, what we do, where we have been. Let's focus on what we can become and how we can accomplish that.

#Story20: The year of rebirth.

A year can truly change a lot. I'm trying to figure out if I changed the year or it changed me...There is still so much to learn but at least, now, I know that there are no winners or losers. We are just doing what we are supposed to do. Sometimes on purpose, sometimes without a purpose. Either way, we all get what we asked for in the end.

#Story21: I'm (not) who I was 10 minutes ago.

This isolation has been intense. Sometimes I feel like it's going way too fast. It feels like I've dissolved most of my former self and I'm slowly becoming one with everything. I no longer identify, title, or label myself with anything. I'm no longer the same person I was 10 minutes ago. My beliefs are no longer constructed and I don't define my existence based on social and cultural conditioning. What is happening?

#Story22: I wasn't who I was.

I started understanding myself only after I completely dissolved myself. Everything that I thought was me, was completely and fully leveled to the ground. Love and light from God raised me from ashes, gifting me with the strongest building blocks as I fully embraced my journey of truth. In the painful process of rebuilding myself, I started realizing who I really was, as my world was no longer based on approximation, orchestrated to serve end-goals driven by dark forces and unknown agendas. My life has finally started making sense to me as I've become one with myself, one with the universe. With God as my guide, love as my drive, and wisdom as my weapon, off I go into a battle against pain and suffering.

*"Everything that I thought
was me, was completely
and fully leveled to
the ground."*

#Story23: "I don't know."

Embrace the "I don't know." When you use this magical phrase, you automatically open yourself up for light to come in. It's positive vulnerability compared to frustration or trying to make up answers when feeling challenged. "I don't know" is knowing that you don't know but it's also knowing that one day you will know. When you say that you don't know, you automatically initiate your growth...That's how simple it can be...

#Story24: Question: How to deal with mean coworkers?

My take on this: To me, it looks like you've entered this job with a certain amount of expectation. You expect to be treated a certain way, to get credit for everything you accomplish, etc. When you don't get acknowledged the way you expect, it creates a battle in your mind, making you believe that everyone may be against you and that you may be failing. My suggestion is that you start focusing on doing a great job and doing it with your whole heart. You're at your job because of your work and not because of your coworkers. Focus on you just doing an amazing job. If after a while you still feel the way you feel, then you should talk to your supervisor. When or if that day comes, the first thing that any supervisor will be looking at is your performance and how passionate you are about it. Nobody will ever go against someone who puts their heart and soul into what they do. Not even your enemies. I'm not eliminating the possibility that your coworkers are actually mean, but you need to be able to recognize what is actually them and what is your own insecurities messing with you. That's your ticket to coming out as a winner each time.

#Story25: Life crisis.

Life crisis, aka self-awakening mechanism, is a reminder that you have been somewhat dishonest with yourself for the first 25-40 years of your life. Luckily, there is no need to worry. Just try to talk to your friends, co-workers, or a family therapist, and with a lot of support and love from them, they can make sure you're back to your programmed factory settings and pretty soon, you can continue living a life that was assigned to you; full of unanswered questions, things you hate to do but you don't know where the hate comes from, people you pretend to like but you don't know why, and the pretend freedom in your hamster-wheel of life. There is no crisis, my friend. It's time to face some long overdue invisible enemies. One at the time. There is no need to rush. One at the time. There is nothing to worry about.

#Story26: Distractions.

Why is a distraction a distraction for you? Maybe it's a distraction because it means something to you? Unless you face it and put some effort in finding out why it creates an emotional experience for you that makes it a priority before other things, you won't be able to stop it from having control over your. You cannot eliminate any distraction without understanding why and how it affects you...

#Story27: Get rid. Eliminate. Establish.

Getting rid of:
Expectations
Secret agendas

In order to help eliminate:
Disappointments
Hurt feelings
Grudges
Frustrations
Anger
Guilt

After establishing:
Boundaries
Communication

#Story28: #rememberliam.

(To my friend Marcus)

The day you lost your son Liam to a drunk driver, I was at a loss for words. At the hospital that night, I was numb because I didn't know what to say. I was embarrassed by my weakness when I saw your strength and goodness as you sat at the bedside by your loving son. I knew that one day I would find the words to tell you all of this, I just didn't know when and how. Marcus, you're a gift to this world. I've been silently following your journey closely ever since and your actions of goodness have spread far and wide. You may not hear it enough and words will never replace Liam, but your way of helping the world by helping others channel out their grief, changing other people's lives for the better, and helping others find their way back after sorrow and suffering, is God's gift. Thank you my friend. #rememberliam

#Story29: Question: Does age difference in couples' matter?

Answer: "The heart wants what the heart wants" right? This may be accurate in theory, but in reality, things may be different. Love doesn't care about age disparities but people certainly do. People obsess over age differences due to the negative stigma that society has regarding it. In general, social structure will most likely force us to subconsciously determine the age difference when people "choose" their partner. Sexual, financial, social, and cultural reasons all play a big role.

So, to answer your question, it depends if you listen to your heart or you're basing your decision when it comes to your partner selection and age based on rational choices and strict analysis of demographic trends and cultural values. What will it be?

"Love doesn't care about age disparities but people certainly do. People obsess over age differences due to the negative stigma that society has regarding it."

#Story30: Live, love, die.

We live, we love, and then we die based on assumptions instead of knowing and feeling. Assumption can be our biggest enemy at times; it's our self-inflicted ignorance based on fear, on not wanting to face what has to be faced in life. We believe it's only enough to see a glimpse in order to know the entire picture. I get asked daily what my thoughts are on life after we die. How can I speak about the afterlife if we barely know anything about this life? Why the rush to skip any steps? Is it your fear, perhaps, that is signaling that you're not living this life to the fullest? Even if you knew the truth, it would not even make sense to you. Try understanding life, by understanding yourself. Then you won't have to ask about what happens after. Death becomes irrelevant because your life becomes relevant.

"We believe it's only enough
to see a glimpse in order
to know the entire picture."

#Story31: Don't push it okay?

Just because something relates to you or to your stage of life, no matter how right it may sound to you or how much you believe it can help someone else only because it helped you, you have no right to push your views, opinions, books, writers, teachings, etc. on others. You may of course present it, but do not end your presentation with: You must try this or there is no other way. Don't, just don't.

#Story32: Relationships.

Relationships are connections between people. We are already all connected with the universal energy; that's why we can understand each other with body language and by evaluating each other's energy that is converted into smiles, laughter, anger, happiness, etc. Every time we feel lonely, we are "forced" to find ways to interact with other people. This doesn't have to be a romantic relationship/connection. If you don't have a need to engage in a romantic relationship with everything that comes with it, you don't have to. Make your relationships and friendships based on depth and not just shallow friendships. When two people meet, they present their best sides of themselves to each other. This is not a relationship but a need for validation. You need to genuinely care and make people open up about their pain, their demons, their true goals, their real problems. The more we make them tell us, the more we will be able to open up about ourselves.

"When two people meet, they present their best sides of themselves to each other. This is not a relationship but a need for validation."

#Story33: We are always where we are supposed to be.

We are always where we are supposed to be, both the wiseman and the fool. What is the difference then? Some people are more aware of it than others. The awareness is a product of our personal connection to our truth. During the first stage of our lives, we deal with confusion and frustration when separating our true nature from what was "forced" on us intentionally or unintentionally and what we adopted without our acknowledgment or awareness (social pressure, parenting, educational institutions, environmental circumstances, media, religion, and culture). Throughout our lives, we constantly get a chance to discover our own truth, our purpose, by finding our way to our actual selves, but unfortunately many people are afraid or simply unable to make a conscious decision to do so.

Some don't even try simply because they love the comfort of their temporary reality they created for themselves or simply because they became a part of someone else's reality without even knowing it. The problem is that our true reality always catches up with us sooner or later. How many times have we heard people who love to play the victim ask: "Oh God, why does this always happen to me?" In that very same question that they ask themselves, they also get the answer to that question and it consists of two words: "Always" and "Me." Don't mix God in it. God always gives us what we ask for. Don't blame God because

we are not aware of the choices we make. Whether we choose to face our own truth or we choose to run away from it, we're always exactly where we are supposed to be every moment of our lives. It's fulfilling and peaceful knowing that we make our choices and our choices don't make us.

"Whether we choose to face our own truth or we choose to run away from it, we're always exactly where we are supposed to be every moment of our lives."

#Story34: Connection to higher powers.

Only you have the power to discover, explore, and define the connection to higher powers and your creator. Other people may show you the door, but only YOU can walk through that door. You also pray and practice on your own terms. Your religious temple is exactly what you define it to be.

The more I'm unfolding my inner/outer discoveries, the more existential correlation and answers I find in literature, art, and mythology that were metaphorically expressed and left behind for us to decode. It's liberating in a way, knowing that there is more in life than just what society has currently adopted as being successful or satisfying.

I will need to dig deeper into their discoveries. Currently, I am trying to restrain myself from reading too much as I try to express my personal discoveries in a raw format when writing it down and then only after, search for material that I can relate it to. I want to finalize at least two books on my own that are completely authentic based on my personal experiences, both inner and outer. This is simply to make the message more relatable to today's generations who no longer find comfort or answers in any of the truth interpretations from the past. On top of that, whenever something is a part of the educational institution, it's widely rejected by young people as they relate that knowledge to the specific teachers who preach it, and their personal qualities and flaws, instead of the information itself.

#Story35: Nothing like my father!

It's only today that I'm brave enough to admit that I've wandered my whole life living in rejection of everything that resembles my father. It's time for me to say farewell to that burden I've carried around for so long. He's a good man. His own pain caused me pain without his ability to fight it. It's okay Dad, I've finally grown into a man strong enough to fight it for both of us. I will now start looking for good in you only. For such a long time, I only looked for reasons to dislike you. Both you and I deserve better. You know Dad, I'm big on love nowadays so here you go, for the first time: I love you Dad.

#Story36: Why can't you be like my mother?

Dear Cat, the vulnerability and fear of being left alone and unprotected as a child was welded into me this whole time. I was so afraid to see my mom go away. The fear became one with me. Its constant release of expectations, resentment, and anger on how you should be blurred my vision so many times, stopped me from seeing all your amazing qualities while expecting myself to see you as another woman who you barely know. It has nothing to do with you. I'm really sorry about all of this. I didn't know, but I know now. I'll make it up to you, I promise. I'm no longer scared. I've grown up now. I need you, my wife, entirely the way you are, my love. You're perfect, you always have been. I can finally see it now. I love you.

#Story37: Question: Can we truly control people?

Answer: Before you read this answer, I'd like you to ask yourself where this question comes from and why. It's that need for control that needs the most attention. Not the actual answer. If you locate the root of it, it will give you all the answers you need. Now, let's look at this interesting perspective. If we look throughout history, legitimate "control" of other humans through a conscious agenda has never really succeeded. Control, as we know it, in the format of having power and unlimited access to people through manipulation of thoughts, emotions, or use of material resources as leverage, is only effective temporarily. Forceful control through physical, mental, or verbal violence towards people whose basic needs depend on them is an act of rooted issues. Whoever tried to consciously manipulate others through rooted blocks, is most likely doomed to wander in their own abyss.

#Story38: Question: Tips on becoming successful?

If you associate success mainly with money and materialism, it's a battle you can never win. Nobody can. Money is about numbers and numbers are infinite and fictional. Define what success means to you based on your personal and realistic definition instead of based off the people around you, people you look up to, and what you believe would make them proud and impressed if you achieved it. Also, detach your definition of success from what is being presented through social media or TV. That type of success is not real. It's an illusion. Success is your personal equilibrium of all the elements that define your entire being. How you get there depends fully on the choices you make.

#Story39: Question: How to maintain focus and motivation when chasing my goals?

Answer: By being true to yourself and by finding your purpose. Remember that your goals are not necessarily what you are supposed to do. You may experience lack of ambition and motivation when working towards your goals. Those may be signals and it's important to take the time to listen to them as your true self may be telling you to change the course of your life and start being more authentic.

"Remember that your goals are not necessarily what you are supposed to do."

#Story40: How to move on from a person you're in love with.

First, you need to define what love means to you. It's important to differentiate it from your habits and needs related to the person you were with and the relationship you built together. If those needs can be covered by another person, then you will be healed from the wounds of your previous relationship as soon as you meet someone else that fits the criteria.

#Story41: Question: How to restart life?

Answer: Let's focus on evolving or transitioning from one phase in life to another. Our life is a collection of all our personal choices combined with what is given to us through genetic inheritance with environmental and social fine-tuning. They contribute to who we are and our life can only evolve into something else as we continuously search for missing answers. Don't forget to stay present as we remind ourselves that life itself is a gift without anything else attached to it.

> *"Don't forget to stay present as we remind ourselves that life itself is a gift without anything else attached to it."*

#Story42: Good & Evil.

Good & evil, darkness &, light, matter & spirit, mind & body are all dualistic concepts of our realities based on individual or shared human experiences. Opposing dualistic powers and their constant interchange are not new concepts in our everyday reality. I no longer look for ways to recognize them or label them, but rather let my introspective energy shifts do the work for me while giving my mind a rest when needed. Certain things are simply above us.

Both good and evil are constantly present within and around us. The difference between them is how you perceive, present, and manifest information, emotions, thoughts, ideas, and teachings. We constantly feed into them, we fight them, we embrace them, we spread them, and project them. Sometimes, evil is packaged and presented as good.

It has helped me find peace to not see myself or the world I live in as a dualistic concept of good and evil, but rather, I try to see myself and the world as one while being aware that in every good, there may be some bad and in every bad, there may be something good. Both when looking outwards and inwards, I no longer try to overanalyze every thought, action, event, person, or situation but rather analyze how my personal peace and balance are affected, including the people that I care about.

"I no longer try to overanalyze every thought, action, event, person or situation, but rather analyze how my personal peace and balance are affected."

#Story43: Experiencing without belonging.

There may be some large misconceptions when it comes to what it truly means to find yourself and get closer to your true self. In today's society, we relate positivity and happiness gained through "success" displayed in a way that our mind can perceive it as valuable. This takes the form of validation, gratification, and materialistic stuff that provides basic physical comfort, shallow friendships, and relationships, so we create a sense of belonging, so we don't feel alone, and to help us escape - like fancy dinners and trips. Those are all experiences in life and they are fine. There is nothing wrong with experiencing life in its various offerings, but losing oneself is easy when falling for experiences, unpacking, and choosing to stay there. One often feels the constant need to feed into the various states that give us a sense of belonging, self-worth, satisfaction, and unfulfilled fulfillment. Finding yourself is the complete opposite. It's about losing the need for all the surface experiences and just being able to be happy and fulfilled in the moment without any external needs. Those needs become optional but we no longer belong to them. They belong to us. It's an inner shift. It's real. It exists.

"There is nothing wrong with experiencing life in its various offerings, but losing oneself is easy while falling for experiences, unpacking, and choosing to stay there."

#Story44: Validation.

I've lived a good portion of my life seeking validation as it definitely serves its purpose. It fills a void and it's a great adrenaline rush when chasing goals and dreams. No doubt it feels good. Things started changing for me when I started asking myself why acceptance and love from complete strangers mattered so much to me. Why was it never enough? Why did it bother me if others, even complete strangers, didn't feed into that need? Why did I see them as instant haters? What was this all about? Questions were many. Answers were few. The more questions I answered for myself, the smaller the need to see myself through the eyes of other people. What a miracle! Could this be the closest to magic I've come to this month? I still find validation to be valid, but only when it's on my terms. No reason to reject it. It exists. It's needed. It's an aid but it's definitely not the cure. Let's be observant.

"Things started changing for me when I started asking myself why acceptance and love from complete strangers mattered so much to me. Why was it never enough?"

#Story45: Question: Are some people unfixable?

Answer: Every person that crosses our path is not supposed to match our speed. Many times, it's a conflict between our agenda and their purpose. Maybe they are not meant to be on any other level than the level they are on. When we experience any sort of frustration related to other people's progress in work, relationships, and other aspects of life, we need to stop and evaluate the entire situation and start asking where the frustration comes from. It's not related to others. Others may only trigger the causes. Instead of repeatedly trying to fix others, let's try to love them for who they are or move on with our lives. Even with family members, it's still the same concept; try to embrace them and love them for who they are, or keep your distance while letting them know that we are here for them if they need us. Let's not forget that many times, while we are asking others to change in order to comfort us, it's actually us who needs healing and it's our own pain that bothers us.

> *"Instead of repeatedly trying to fix others,*
> *let's try to love them for who they are,*
> *or move on with our lives."*

#Story46: Question: Are you happy with your wife?

Answer: My wife is not responsible for my satisfactory perception of her. The day I realized that my happiness with my wife had a lot to do with my own wounds, imbalances, and personal needs was the day I stopped putting pressure on her to feed into my emotional states. Something within me shifted that day. I started seeing qualities in her that I wasn't able to see before as my own wounds didn't let me see beyond their needs. It's a process, my friends, and a continuous path of growth, but it always starts with introspective analysis.

#Story47: Question: What do you want for Christmas?

Answer: I want people to pause in the middle of the holiday hysteria and ask themselves two questions:

1. Why am I even buying all this junk? Is it really going to make up for all the time I didn't spend with the person, all the calls I didn't make, and texts I didn't reply because I simply don't even know why I didn't do those things?

2. What would happen if I don't buy anything for anyone this year but instead, just take this money and buy some pen and paper and write down some reflections of my life and on life in general - Where have I been? What am I doing? Where am I going? Who am I? Who are the people I'm going to give all this junk to? Do I even know my kids, my friends, my parents? Do I truly know their battles, their pain, their desires? Are they happy? What is this all about? Could this be something else?

#Story48: Emotion or Logic?

Dualism at its finest. Why see them as separate entities? They should work seamlessly together each time we are faced with any decision making. Any decision that is made solely by our left, more pragmatic and logical side of the brain, or solely by our right side, connected to our heart's wants and needs, will lead to imbalances in our life. Emotions drive most of the choices we make, but our mind is rarely aware of it. At this stage of my life, I go with decisions that give me most balance and peace. That's a personal compass I trust more than playing a guessing game that creates a battle between my emotions and logic.

> *"Emotions drive most of the choices we make but our mind is rarely aware of it."*

#Story49: I setup my own geographical trap.

I never felt like I belonged anywhere I lived or visited. I decided to go west, as west as I could. From Europe to LA, and I found what I needed for about a year. When the novelty and excitement wore off, I felt the same old unsatisfactory feeling creep in from nowhere, but this time it was different. This time, I was alone. No family and no real friends around me while constantly surrounded by people, but always feeling lonely. Where should I go now? I was ready to give up and go back defeated while not even knowing what beat me. As my mind descended into a gloomy darkness, an angel from heaven entered my life and she introduced me to love. I always believed that cats were mysterious but this Cat I met didn't bring any mysteries with her. This Cat helped me solve them all...Maybe it wasn't about places after all. It's about the world that we create. It's either built on love or built on chaos.

"Maybe it wasn't about places after all.
It's about the world that we create."

#Story50: Minimalistic illusion.

My needs have become minimal but my choices and actions in life have created possibilities for me. Having ambition to create in life doesn't make us a profligate. The goal should be to achieve a level of self-actualization and awareness where your drive for creating and building no longer comes from a place of greed, fear, or outer world expectations, but rather from a place of knowing your purpose and knowing why and what you are building. If I chose materialistic minimalism just to make a statement, it would become an agenda and yet another imbalance to deal with.

#Story51: Greed vs. Ambition.

To create with an ambition that comes from a place of pure intent and from a place of personal balance, is positive ambition. Creating from a place of desire for personal power, conquest, lust, hidden desires, and agendas, or from a place of financial and social unfulfillment is greed.

#Story52: Chasing gets exhausting.

Sometimes I wonder why so many see happiness and success as some sort of a goal that you must chase. The chase itself often leads to more unhappiness and less success. I just wish that more people could try to embrace their entire existence as happiness and success, and extract their strength from it, while allowing themselves to be in the moment. There is so much beauty in it.

#Story53: How do we unlearn something?

When we keep our minds open to new information, we absorb knowledge that makes more sense to us than what we have previously known. Our minds overwrite what we know or expand. Unlearning is really about evolving and not about undoing ourselves. When we absorb new and fresh information that is aligned with our path and also with the truth, we just experience it as an "aha, it totally makes sense" moment.

> *"Unlearning is really about evolving and not about undoing ourselves."*

#Story54: Where we are is not who we are.

There is a reason why we all are where we are. But who we are and where we are, isn't the entire truth about us. If you are reading this book, it probably means that you are seeking more in life. That "more" is your desire to make personal changes and growth because something within you is driving you towards that search. It doesn't matter where that desire comes from. It's important that it exists. Your search and desire for growth is growth itself. You are constantly making progress and changes that you may not always be aware of. They don't always have to be major changes. The physical manifestation of your growth in your journey always comes after your inner shift. Trust the process and trust the powers above us. God always meets us halfway.

"Your search and desire for growth is growth itself."

#Story55: Passions, E-Motions, Virtues, Love.

Every intense enthusiasm must have an origin. Does it matter what the origin is? Not unless it interferes with your day-to-day life. Fear, hatred, joy, sadness, wonder, lust, anger, and jealousy are all instinctive and genetically inherited lower energy passions that trigger emotions. Emotions make our body react, and they keep us going. Our primitive instincts are counterbalanced with higher energy points through virtues. I've identified Love to be in the middle of it all as the main energy point that balances the entire equation.

"Our primitive instincts are counterbalanced with higher energy points through virtues."

#Story56: Questioning the unquestionable.

I question everything that I see, hear, or feel daily that has an impact on changing or shaping my life, while accepting everything as it is. The questions I ask myself are: Can this be something else? Is there truth present in this? If I don't find better answers, then I'm where I'm supposed to be for the moment.

#Story57: Archetypes & its construct.

At times throughout this journey, I have had this immense sense of being special for my personal discoveries and insights. Luckily, my awareness doesn't let me celebrate for too long as each discovery leads me to my "predecessors" and their attempts to answer the same questions I have. Today, it's obvious to me that universal fundamental characteristics were imprinted on us before we were even born. Through my intense and raw conversations with my beloved followers through social media from all walks of life, it's obvious that there is a universal subconscious behavioral pattern. The pattern itself is a spiritual construct and it's as real to me as the physical body. No matter how much I search, it all leads to love as the fundamental base of it all.

It feels safe and promising. We are not alone, there is a higher power watching over us. All we really have to do is to try to tune in to those vibrations of the universal patterns. It's a blissful experience and we need to take a break here and there from our everyday stress and routines.

"No matter how much I search,
it all leads to love as the
fundamental base of it all."

#Story58: The Journey.

Twelve months of my interstellar travel and search I have faced the following:
1. Face to face with the Devil
2. From chains to wings
3. The Search
4. Travel & Turbulent Landing
5. Joy, Confusion, Decisions
6. The Brink Of Tragedy
7. Rebirth
8. Integration
9. Philanthropy

#Story59: Be different.

What's different? What is one's point of reference when evaluating and perceiving what being different is? It's the need for being different that I'd like to look at. Where does the need come from? Being authentic is what happens when our need for being different stops.

#Story60: Question: What would you tell someone that hates herself?

Answer: You don't hate yourself, you hate the person that people made you believe that you are.

Hate is a sum of emotions that we acquire throughout life from different people, society, and our upbringing. Life experiences and people that hurt us build up strong and hidden emotional layers. They can be hate, anger, depression, anxiety, lack of ambition or hyper ambition. They lead to clogged energy within ourselves that acts as heavy anchors, stopping us from functioning properly and having a fulfilling life.

I suggest you initiate a (true) self-discovery journey that leads to personal growth. Make it your priority. Find yourself first and see how you feel about yourself. You may discover a lot of different things, but hate for yourself doesn't come from our core being. It doesn't come from our higher essence. You absorbed it from others. Get rid of those layers and find love for your true self. Reset yourself to emotional "factory settings" and from there, add layers of everything that you are.

#Story61: Creativity.

Creativity originates from authenticity. Originality lies in the origins of your true essence. In order to access it, you'll need to burn away some of those layers of masks that you have adopted by people, social norms, and social situations that you surround yourself with. When you are motivated by creativity, you no longer have the desire to compete with others. Others will have no ability to compete with your originality. No matter what they see on the surface, they will never be able to envision anything beyond your presentation. The visible is the manifestation of the invisible. If your creativity comes from the invisible, the visible will be extraordinary.

"When you are motivated by creativity, you no longer have the desire to compete with others. Others will have no ability to compete with your originality."

#Story62: L E A - Love - Expression - Attention

It's evident that basic psychological and physical survival needs such as food, drink, shelter, clothing, warmth, sex, sleep, protection and stability are no longer enough in today's society to be able to live a balanced life or achieve a sense of fulfillment and happiness.

Love, expression, and attention are important, basic elements that I've incorporated in the basic survival needs when approaching my parenting role. An absence of those emotions during childhood may result in imbalances that subconsciously forces kids to seek to compensate for the voids, through self-destructive habits, reality escapes, and behaviors that harm themselves and others.

As I'm implementing this philosophy in my parenting approach, I make my own discoveries and personal darkness that I have to face. We truly have so much to learn from and through our children.

"Love, expression, and attention are important basic elements that I've incorporated in the basic survival needs when approaching my parenting role."

#Story63: Indoctrination.

When people speak of education, they think of degrees before they think of knowledge and they are not wrong. Knowledge is something we discover on our own, as nobody can give you knowledge without your consent. Education can give you instructions, guidance, and teach you patterns of how things work when preparing for work life. A degree serves as a passport to get you into the workforce where you further your skills and ability in your professional life. Knowledge, wisdom, and personal growth should always be a side gig in every stage of our life.

"When people speak of education, they think of degrees before they think of knowledge and they are not wrong."

#Story64: Question: How to step out of your comfort zone?

Answer: By stepping into some discomfort. All you truly need is one simple step. The rest will be easy. Nothing is as hard as taking a cold morning shower after you have showered for years with warm water. You think it's easy? Just go ahead and try it and do some analysis of that ritual. It's not just a shower. It's your personal morning ritual, your meditation, where you are stepping out of something extremely comfortable into something extremely uncomfortable. It will set the tone for your entire day and week. Making those extra phone calls, doing more work, emails, planning your future, and dealing with unpleasant people will appear as a piece of cake once you complete your first cold shower. It will open a whole new gateway of possibilities and fresh confidence. You will walk around thinking like a superhuman. Nothing is as tough as taking that cold shower after a night of warm, cozy sleep. If you do that three times a week, you will be able to do anything. It's all about changing the energy patterns and not falling back into the same old routine.

#Story65: Don't train your mind. It's not your pet.

"Train your mind to be stronger than your emotions." I see this (new-age) phrase posted around the Internet and can't help but dissect it to check for any substantial value. This phrase is as processed and synthetic as any other fast food nowadays. And just like fast food, this phrase has very low nutritional value in it, but it tastes good. The danger of synthetic wisdom is causing people to build additional layers of distance between them and their truth. Every time you try to "train" your mind, you're becoming more computerized. Your brain is a processor - it works for you and your brain will do whatever you tell it to, regardless if it's wrong or right.

You don't train your brain; it's not your pet. You don't feed your brain with false phrases (programs); it's not one of your apps. You also don't make parts of yourself compete with each other. By doing so, you're just pushing away your pain and imbalances by masking them. Your emotions are not going anywhere, no matter how much you try to train your brain to undermine your emotional importance. The only way to make your emotions work for you is by letting them resurface; by facing them and acknowledging them and by making them irrelevant and powerless. Trying to shut down your emotions is like babysitting a crying child and instead of finding out what is wrong, you lock the child in a dark room and you put earplugs in to drown out the noise. This is not a good scenario. When it comes to personal development, make sure to question what is being put out there nowadays. No matter who shares it or who's behind it, just remember that most people are just trying to fix themselves while they sell solutions to others, while searching for validated value in what they offer to others.

"The only way to make your emotions work for you is by letting them resurface; by facing them and acknowledging them and by making them irrelevant and powerless."

#Story66: Can a person change you?

We can learn and grow from pretty much every person that we meet. This is only possible if we learn how to bypass the guards that stand in between us and our growth. The guards are our EGO and our INSECURITIES. With that said, another person can never change you unless you are open for change. You may have the most enlightened person as your guide, but you will always be the one who needs to walk through the door of personal progress.

The opposite can occur when we have multiple imbalances and insecurities that can lead to us attracting people who are similar to us. Once we are grouped with them, we tend to stagnate in growth and even regress as we use those people as a reference of what is "normal" or "average" but the reality is something different. The less aware you are, the more negative impact others may have on you without your knowledge.

#Story67: Why do we sometimes feel discontent with ourselves?

Answer: Because distraction is always packaged as something beautiful or presented as something that makes us feel that it is better than what we have or who we are. When "that" takes our attention away from ourselves, our nature or our family, we become discontent and disconnected from the truth, and from ourselves while chasing something that doesn't exist. We become slaves/robots serving a purpose that is not our own.

#Story68: Emotional deformities.

Emotional deformities are equivalent to physical deformities. It's Nature's rejection of the human attempt to go against or across the blueprint patterns that were set for us. Some are genetic, some are environmental, and some are a mix of both.

#Story69: Networking or flex of egos?

Networking: a gathering of people looking for answers in life disguised as "got it all figured out" and successful individuals. They share their amazing stories with others without realizing how they build walls of emptiness each time they open their mouth, not letting any valuable information into their empty souls. Everyone leaves with fewer answers than before, wondering if they did well and if they impressed others.

#Story70: What books are the right books?

Books should be used as references for self-reflection and not as the main source for one's growth. First, you need to initiate a self-discovery phase. It's a phase where you start pinpointing what you are trying to fix. Focus on one or two major issues at a time. Once you know what you need to overcome, you can start looking for solutions. Regardless if you search in books, movies, conversations with other people, gurus, or speakers, you'll need to go through the motions of life and experience life in order for you to relate to or determine the authenticity of other scripts and teachings.

#Story71: Question: How to deal with the fear of losing someone you love?

Answer: This fear is rooted and it is hard to locate its origins. It is related to safety and protection. It is most likely related to the fear of abandonment in childhood. A child being left for too long crying and unsupervised can imprint memories and fear in the subconscious mind that later in life can resurface as fear of losing people that are close to them. Another example is, a child who is constantly present in adult discussions about death and violence, can develop an exaggerated fear of death and violence as a grownup as a result. If children are in violent and abusive environments growing up, they might be involved in one as an adult.

When people are in the process of shaping their identity and finding their truth, they are fragile and strongly dependent on the love of other people. The thought of losing someone close is frightening. It's very common and almost everyone has to go through it at some point. Try searching for a deeper meaning of life and not just see it as a straight line with a beginning and ending. It's important to be able to separate a real life threat to those we love from rooted fear that is not real.

#Story72: Fear of failure. Pressure.

Another rooted one. Someone close to you fed your fragile mind as a child with programs and false fear, containing a list of things that could happen to you if you didn't do as instructed. The fear is not real, my friend. You'll have to track it down and cut it by its root. The fear puts pressure on you to perform beyond what is necessary.

Why would you let yourself be defined by your achievements, what you do, what you wear, or how much you make? None of those things can promise us tomorrow. Every person is more than that.

There is too much pressure on students. If they score low on a test or fail one thing, they perceive it as a catastrophe. Education should be fun and enjoyed. The learning process should matter more than passing a test. Students undergo the process of sacrifice, hard work, and not living in order to find what they believe is the formula for happiness. Parents replace love with activities to try to help their kids get ahead. It's time to take a step back, take a deep breath, and rethink our priorities and what life is truly all about. Happiness is here and now. The future will create itself if we find a way to see the value of being present.

Learning should enrich every person's life. It shouldn't take away the joy by creating blinders.

#Story73: You can't offend me with judgments.

In order for me to be offended, I must identify with the subject that carries the offense attempt. If my wounds are healed, your words can't even reach me as they have nothing to stick to. They may only return to you and to the place of your own projections as I let you implode in it. Remember that every word you speak that has no truth about me is only a judgment, and each word will display your own emotional profile and tell a story about your entire life. Be careful what you throw at others on the Internet as it will always find you. That's how it works my friend.

#Story74: What Is EXISTENCE?

Our world and life (existence) is a constant harmonious play of two opposing energies. Every thought you initiate, the universe (God/Higher power) will answer through different ways to balance out what you just initiate with your thinking. Our thinking is the beginning of one's manifestation. It's a simple, yet one of the most complex mathematical equations. What exactly does this mean? Whatever a person thinks or does will affect that person the most regardless of the person's intentions...

But what's the meaning of life? Does it even have one? Or what's the purpose of us humans even existing? What happens after we die?

I believe that those who find those answers are not supposed to tell other people, but rather guide them to their own answers.

#Story75: De-Press-Ion.

De - Removal

Press - Pressure

Ion - (imbalance) a positive or negative electric charge as a result of having lost or gained one or more electrons.

Depression is your inner self telling you that you need to look into ways of removing some of the pressure from yourself that may be creating an internal imbalance. It's your inner self protecting you from future fatalities and havoc. Your spirit sees what your eyes don't. Never see depression as an end but rather, a chance for a new beginning. Give yourself a chance to live a life that you were meant to live and not a life that you believed you were supposed to live. Your life is your life. You are more than what the world sees on the surface. Your life is more than what you see on the surface.

#Story76: Is ignorance bliss?

Silent ignorance is bliss.
Loud ignorance is destructive.

#Story77: En(LIE)ghtenment.

Many of you have been sending me quotes and other texts to dissect and evaluate. You recognize that something is off and you seek my opinion. We have had fun with it many times while decoding lies, false prophecies, and programmed wisdom. I'll make it easy for all of you to recognize truth from lies without giving it too much thought. If any individual who sells wisdom is not ready to put themselves out there, stripped down naked to their bare soul in front of all of their followers, I'm afraid they dilute truth with personal issues. Distorted truth is a harmful force. If embraced fully without your ability to rationalize the message, this may make you feel that you are doing everything wrong in life. Truth is brutal, but it always has light and hope in it.

*"Truth is brutal but it always
has light and hope in it."*

#Story78: Mommy & Daddy issues.

Mommy and Daddy issues form when one of the parents is prevented from fulfilling their parenting roles. Identity crisis, abandonment fear, sexual and love attachments based on emotional states, are some of the issues that follow men and women in early adulthood. For boys, an emotional and physical absence of their mothers trigger them to seek replacements as grownups. For girls, the absence of their fathers may force them to search for men who can fill the void from their childhood rather than being with a man who's right for them.

Men with Daddy issues result in identity crisis and the same with women and Mommy issues.

#Story79: Women with Daddy issues.

"Daddy issues" is an urban/slang phrase describing psychological aspects behind a young woman's romantic behavior. It's related to a father figure and his partial or entire physical and emotional absence during her early days of childhood.

Safety, protection, love, care, and basic survival, are all recorded within energies of one's roots. These memories create subconscious behavioral patterns later on in life. A young woman unknowingly confuses being in love with feeding into subconscious memories when she, for example, meets a married man with children. She has no ability to fight the temptation that is being presented as a "loving and caring father" and she fiercely defends his actions of cheating on his spouse with irrational thinking. Men who feed into this phenomenon become victims as well, as they often seek approval and love from younger women once they pass a certain age, but still haven't solved all their insecurities.

#Story80: Men with Daddy issues.

I call them Daddy issues because they start in early childhood. In men, this is related to our identity. A man with daddy issues rejects his father, his attributes, achievements, and seeks a path in life that is the opposite of his father. Resentment, anger, hurt, and denial follow him into adulthood as heavy chains and dictate major life-decisions. As long as we battle with those issues, we will be possessed by them until peace is achieved.

#Story81: Life can only be experienced.

Life can't be purchased. Life must be experienced. To experience swimming in a lake, one must go out in nature, into the lake - one can't bring it into the office, or just read about it in a book. To experience the smell, taste, and feeling of a fresh authentic hotdog, even a billionaire can't accomplish that by buying a hot dog stand. Life can ONLY be experienced. Life can't be simulated.

#Story82: Sacrifice is success, not sacrifice.

A personal sacrifice that serves my family and brings me closer to them is never a sacrifice. It's a personal accomplishment, a battle won and a step closer to my truth. Seeing it as a sacrifice is just our mind playing tricks on us, trying to create emotional layers of self-pity, martyrdom, and self-inflicted pain. Releasing myself from everything that stands in between my family and what's best for them is exactly how things are supposed to be. The rest will fall into place.

#Story83: So why do we have prisons if what people did in the past doesn't matter?

Only because a battle in the physical world against dark forces is lost, it doesn't mean that life is over. Some people who lack the strength and ability to fight properly against the darkness and certain issues need time away for their own protection and protection of others. It doesn't mean that people can't grow under those circumstances. People make mistakes, but we never know what God's plan is for everyone. Prisons are not only physical guards, but they are actually guards of bad energy that happened to occupy the bodies of those who are jailed. They too can change and find strength, even in prison. They find their peace by freeing themselves from the darkness. Even though they are physically jailed, they can still be emotionally and mentally free. The past can't be changed. Our spiritual, mental, and emotional states can.

> *"The past can't be changed.*
> *Our spiritual, mental, and*
> *emotional states can."*

#Story84: Letting go of the past.

All the crap from your past doesn't matter as it wasn't really you. It was you fighting against who you weren't. The latest and the most updated version of yourself is here and now. Let go of all the guilt, blame, and hate towards everyone else and towards yourself as everyone is fighting the same things at different phases of their life. Let go of bad thoughts and emotions and watch yourself be filled with an immense sense of your importance in life.

#Story85: Letting go vs. forgiveness.

Letting Go = Forgiveness with understanding of what we are forgiving. Forgiveness alone may of course, work temporarily, but there could still be some emotional strings attached. Without fully cutting them off, the past can still hunt us down when our guard is low. I'd prefer if people try to locate the cause and cut it off by its roots, so it can't attack them again. That could manifest in "letting go" and a complete emotional release of some major issues and heavy chains that hold us down.

#Story86: Humanity against issues, not humanity against people.

I truly wish that this concept catches fire. Can we try to understand that most of the time, it's humanity against darkness, against mental issues; and not humanity against individuals or groups of people? I see myself as someone who would like to help people understand where some of the pain and suffering comes from.

#Story87: Parenting through guidance.

Using discipline in parenting is easy. Using guidance that involves patience and being present requires love. We listen, observe, guide, present options, and show our daughter the world through books. We have frequent family meetings usually by doing art with her and we ask her how we can be better parents. If she does something wrong, it's because she is only six, and to her, it's right; so we sit down to explain how it can be bad for her or others. Grownups need discipline. Children need guidance.

"Using discipline in parenting methods is easy. Using guidance that involves patience and being present requires love."

#Story88: How to know our children more?

By being present and available. Not just physically, but emotionally too. We need to give them our time instead of things. Kids only need our love, our guidance, and our protection. Everything else we give them is to make us feel good about ourselves. That's not what they need. We always need to pay attention to what they say and how they say it. Gaining their trust is not as easy as we think it is. When they invite us into their world, we need to enter it and stay there with them. If they don't trust us, they will create their own emotional world within themselves, and when that happens, we never know what type of an emotional maze they may enter and how that will affect them when they grow up.

#Story89: Our children are a fountain of light.

As I've mentioned before, our kids are a never ending source of knowledge for us adults. One of the latest lessons from my daughter arrived in the form of a joke. She knows more jokes than any other human being I've ever met and they are all so creative and wise, yet so innocent.

Layla: "Dad, imagine you are trapped in a house with no windows or doors, how do you get out?"

Me: "Hmm I don't know."

Layla: "You get out by stopping imagining!"

All of us can learn from that - when faced with an imaginary unsolvable problem, or some daunting challenge we've created in our own mind...just stop imagining!

#Story90: Our children are mirrors of our soul.

Having kids, or even just being around kids, is a privilege and a chance for us adults to elevate our personal growth in ways we can only imagine.

Life may be an unexplainable miracle that we try to understand daily, but creating a life gives us a chance to witness that wonder from the very beginning. Being a parent has truly helped me understand life and better myself on so many levels, while giving me a new path to finding my balance. As soon as I realized that my daughter's happiness, overall well-being, creativity, and self-esteem, would be nothing else but a reflection of my own well-being, I no longer had excuses for myself.

We prepare for so many things in life but being a parent is something we evolve into. It's hard to know what the right thing to do is all the time, but all we can do is to do our best. We try to put a smile on our little girl's face as much as we can, and that is somewhat a measure of how well we do as parents. The beautiful moments that are created and shared together are what truly matters and we try to create those every day, regardless of whether they are a bedtime story or a walk in the neighborhood.

#Story91: Let's guide our children instead of programming them to obey.

Our children don't need to be told what to do. They don't need grownups to exercise their power and project their insecurities on the most fragile, vulnerable, and innocent souls on earth. They need a lot of love, a lot of care, protection, and guidance; they need us to listen to them when they speak, when they sing, and when they cry. They need us to let them be kids and let them dream without our interference. Our children are our world, our future, and the answer to all the questions you may have about life. They are not our escape from life. They are our life. Start seeing and treating them that way.

#Story92: To all the mothers out there.

Your ability to deliver a new soul into this world is one of the greatest contributions to humanity. You temporarily give up parts of your life and your body, but know that you also contribute to the world in a way that only a woman can. If you look at your babies in the eyes, what you'll see is them staring at their hope for the future. Your strength is their strength. It's a miracle right before you, and you'll be rewarded in ways you never imagined were possible. Your confidence and will power will slowly grow back to newer and greater heights. What you're experiencing is growth and you're getting closer to discovering your purpose in life. Celebrate every second.

#Story93: Father guilt.

As a father, there were many times I was so focused on creating this magical world for my baby girl that I failed to realize I was all the magic she truly needed and wanted. I was trying to eliminate the guilt of not being there for her by bribing her with fancy presents and things that created excitement for her for a few hours, when all she really wanted was me just being there, listening to her, understanding her thoughts, being a part of her magical world, and making everything around her alive. We sometimes fail at listening to understand, and instead, just listen so we have a proper reply. Father's Day is most likely just another holiday created by some father out of pure guilt for not being there for his kids. We need to make every day Father's Day, otherwise, it may be too late one day, and no gifts, holidays, words and even our time will be enough to compensate for not being there when we were truly needed. Layla, sorry for not knowing better before, but I'm here now baby girl.

#Story94: Men and women.

Without necessarily changing your point of view, let's try to understand the concept of man and woman and the fact that both genders have strengths that the opposite sex doesn't. If we focus on the strengths of each gender, and celebrate those while embracing the thought that those differences in genders exist for a reason, it becomes easier to see that those differences balance us out.

There is no battle - men vs. women. Let's fight against problems, not against each other. Let's fight for love, for our children, for life, for our future, and let's fight against issues that stand between us. It's about balance. We need balance. Embracing and celebrating differences while trying to exclude personal hurts, projections, needs, or views can be healthy and liberating.

#Story95: Question: Are men smarter than women?

Answer: Men and women are different, they complement each other, and they should never be compared in any way - intellectually, spiritually, and physically. The beauty of human nature is that men and women are complex in equal measures and they are both gifted with different abilities to help them fulfill complementary roles within society and individual journeys.

#Story96: Being and becoming a man.

In today's society, it's very confusing and difficult knowing how to be a man. Any attempt to carve out our manhood as we know it, that involves masculinity in its original biological format may put us at risk of being labeled as socially "unfit." But then again, what is biological anyway? How do we know that those attributes that have been assigned to us throughout history haven't been distorted or manipulated the same way as today's social pressures and agendas try to dictate how a man should be? Throughout my journey, I've gone through several phases and dimensions, both physical and mental; as a jacked bodybuilder, a loving father and husband, a stressed out businessman, an anxious pretend grownup who never took the time to face my rooted issues, to my current state of a somewhat balanced individual who's entering a new phase of life, living life fully on my terms while seamlessly integrating all aspects of life and society.

So what does being a man mean to me? It's a frequency. A frequency that gives me the most peace, health, and balance while not neglecting any obligations or responsibilities towards nature, society, and most importantly my family. Once I realized this and once I started following my inner compass while using the outer world as the mirror for self-reflection,

everything started changing. I'm no longer affected by what anyone tries to introduce or push onto me. All those things are just attempts from others to
impose their agendas upon me. It doesn't concern me. My personal peace and balance comes first. If that is disrupted, I'm letting myself fall into simulations and lies. Being and becoming a man is a journey. We are only born with 50%. The next 50% is a search.

"Being and becoming
a man is a journey,
we are only
born with 50%.
The next 50%
is a search."

#Story97: True power.

Our true power comes from us knowing our bigger purpose. That's when your warrior spirit gets support from everyone and everything around you. Your enemies become your supporters without them even knowing it. Our drive to create, build, live, love, and give, comes from a place of purity, the right intentions, and awareness that you belong to something much greater than what everything appears to be. That's the only true power there is.

#Story98: Disagreements.

Disagreements never have to become arguments. They only become arguments when a person starts involving personal opinions and unhealed wounds that act as constructs in their own matrix and only exist in their own head (universe). Exit your matrix and enter the universe. Try to practice focusing on this awareness with one argument or disagreement and see what happens!

#Story99: Evolved perception made me stronger.

It's not strength that makes us stronger; it's evolved perception. Finding a way to change the way we perceive reality leads to emotional balance, healing, and healthy channeling of negative energy. Being strong is not your ability to block things or people out or just blocking your emotions. Being strong is about you seeing things the way they truly are and not the way you feel about them. That is what true strength is and that's the path to your inner equilibrium.

It's not strength that makes us stronger;
it's evolved perception.

#Story100: I'm on this path.

I'm on this path. It's empty, but I do see traces of faded footprints. It's quiet, but I hear lost voices behind me trying to find their way. It's peaceful, but the silence scares me slightly. It's scary, but harmony is guiding me with stories and information that were not accessible to me before. There are crossroads, but the main road is beautiful - it's clear and it's giving me direction to where I'm supposed to continue. There is no speed limit, but I'm not tempted to run. I see no end, but the glow ahead is the most beautiful I've ever seen. I take a deep breath as my entire being is filled with a tingly feeling that I recognize clearly, a vibration of truth that took me to this path. The voices behind me are more intense, they are more clear. They finally see me and I see them slowly exiting the off-roading as they are joining me on this path.

#Story101: To My Dear Wife: The night I said goodbye to an old friend.

My love,

Tonight as I step into another milestone, infused with light and love from God while still being an old friend of darkness and a new child of light, I wanted to remind myself of all the reasons that I should celebrate this evening with you. I'm dissolving my demons into the eternity of no return with a mixture of my new consciousness as I elevate myself, with you by my side. Watch me extract toxicity as I convert it into rays of light while reminding myself of the gift I was given. I love you and thank you for being by my side on my journey. Without you, I would be dancing with the devil.

"Darkness is the only place where the truth can grow strong without the interference of those who fear it and seek to destroy it. Only purity has the courage to enter pathways that lead to the core of the truth of our creation where our purpose serves as the secret key, unlocking the gates of truth whose divine brightness spreads its rays of life that are necessary for human existence and survival."

#Story102: Self-made.

Being self-made is a very cool and widely encouraged success concept nowadays that promises freedom while rarely realizing the trap of self-imposed enslavement of personal freedom. Aren't we all self-made anyway? We use different formats and frameworks to accomplish similar goals. Peek behind the curtain before you sign up for anything.

#Story103: Gut - Heart - Mind.

Gut - Heart - Mind = The Holy Trinity of your decision making. They are all equally important and they should all be equally trusted in order for you to accomplish a well-balanced life that leads to fulfillment. None of them should have an authoritative right to *decide* for you but they should all *work together* for you.

#Story104: Cheating in pain.

Cheating is deeply rooted issues that trigger people to seek ways to fill a void through multiple sexual encounters with strangers and people who are not their partner. It's a blind search for "something" without having any clue what that something is. It's not about sex - especially since masturbation gives equal or better pleasure than sex without emotional connection. Sex is just a "trap" that is easy to fall into. Lust is not an easy enemy. There are no winners in cheating scenarios, other than lust itself. This topic must be approached with caution and without judgment. Only then, will there be an environment where answers may appear.

"There are no winners in cheating scenarios, other than lust itself."

#Story105: Coitus reservatus and celibacy.

My announcement about my sex celibacy on my social media was one of the most interesting, emotional, and thought provoking triggers that I have ever experienced throughout my search. Every person that gave feedback had a strong opinion about it. All valuable and valid, but not a single person seemed to have the ability to objectively evaluate a possible purpose behind my actions without mixing in their personal opinions, wounds, desires, or personal experiences. I have answered over 10,000 questions through my social media stories, occasionally pushing some people into interesting dimensions, but most people were able to tackle them. SEX celibacy was something different. It was strong, it was personal, it was emotional, it was provoking, it was comforting, it was wrong, it was right, it was spiritual, it was evil, it would destroy my marriage, it would make it stronger. Some even "ordered" me to keep my "experiment" to myself. It's absolutely intriguing how easy it becomes to evaluate our entire society and our ability to see beyond personal opinions once we incorporate such an intimate and strong energy vortex such as sexual energy. I was only searching for one answer with my celibacy that I initiated without any definite duration.

My goal was simply to find an answer. In a marriage such as mine, where sex has played an important part from the very first date, I was simply seeking to see how my feelings towards my wife and how our
connection to each other would be affected if sex was completely and mutually eliminated from our marriage. I got my answers. I also see no reason to tell you how long my celibacy lasted or what answers I discovered. I do not want anyone to mimic this part of the journey as this is intimate and personal and it's something that needs to be explored without anyone's interference. I believe that this story has given you the right tools to initiate and finalize this specific part of your journey if you evaluate that it's needed in your relationship or marriage.

#Story106: Release the tease.

This is my answer to a follower who has a professional career, but is looking to do a live webcam appearance and asked me for my opinion:

"I sense a certain level of inadequate fatherly presence, attention, and love when you were younger. You now look to compensate for that by playing the role of a "tease" through live webcam while justifying it as a need for a side-job. I'm afraid that that type of "love" may leave you even more empty. I apologize in advance for a possible emotional rush from your side. I could also be wrong with my evaluation and in that case, you can disregard my message, but I did feel a certain level of freedom to present my thoughts since you were so blunt. I assume that this will not be an issue and I hope that the answer helps you."

#Story107: An awakening agenda is still an agenda.

Pushing for an "awakening" agenda puts us in the same category as any other mind manipulation. We can only be light for others, but we should NEVER cause damage by forcing light into the eyes of those who have found their peace in their own world.

What I share with you is no different from the way anyone else would share their own thoughts and discoveries about life. I expect no one to adopt anything or change their lives in any way. I can just hope that some of you may find something helpful in what I've chosen to write and share. My life is no more authentic or exciting than anyone else's life. It's just different, but so is your life...

"My words are only loud to those who allow them to be loud. I'm not able to speak louder, because if I did it would be shouting out nonsense."

#Story108: Sexelligence.

Sexual energy is the most powerful energy we have. Through sexual intercourse, the sexual energy moves and starts circulating. By circulating sexual energy through the heart (having consensual sex with the person you love), sex becomes more profound, healing and spiritual. Healing sexual energy becomes principle and creates more balance and harmony. If sexual energy is used primarily as a release through irresponsible sex, it only serves as a primal energy that bypasses the heart (which is the center of our well-being) and it reaches our higher energy levels in its primal form, where it can affect our balance, emotional well-being, and create other emotional and mental imbalances leaving us with a feeling of emptiness.

People need to start seeing sex as a serious, intimate, and a powerful life force. A force that can create life, but also a force that can destroy life as well.

#Story109: Question: How did you know that your wife was the one?

I did not know. All I knew was that when I met her, every other woman started fading away into the background. For the first time, I started leaving my phone unlocked and it felt so good and so right. I knew that she was able to bring out this side of me that I really liked and I wanted to see that side of me daily. I was able to be completely myself, for the first time, without the need to be anything or anyone else, when I was with her. I also knew that the feelings I was developing for her were deep, real, honest, and I knew that the connection we were experiencing was on a different level. I did not know what it was about her or about us. I did not know many things and I chose to not overthink it, but I knew that I wanted to explore all of it with her.

Now 10 years later, I feel that I'm slowly getting some of the answers that I couldn't figure out in the beginning. I also now realize that I wasn't supposed to know some of the answers back then. I was supposed to live and to experience life with my wife and not try to know or understand.

"I was able to be completely myself for the first time
without the need to be anything or anyone
else but myself when I was with her."

#Story110: Healing Love.

A Woman's love is the mightiest healing force in the world. It's our gateway, our passage, and the key to the source of everything that causes us pain, but we are the only ones who can make it all go away by feeding into that love. The more fuel we give her to make her love stronger for us, the faster and the closer we get to the epicenter of our own internal strength. That's where we can make the shift of our internal powers. That's where we can turn off the pain, the darkness, our deepest nightmares and everything we feel is wrong about us. Once the love is so strong that you completely heal, you may experience this release of bright energy that is perceived as positivity, understanding, and unconditional love; not just for people that are close to you, but even for people that can't do anything for you. If you don't already have that woman in front of you, I'd open all my senses, so when the day comes when you meet that woman, I would suggest you be very selective with how you treat her, how you love her, how you listen to her, how you make her feel, and also how you react and care when you don't make her feel the way she should. That woman can be your key to becoming the person you always wanted to become, but she will not be able to do it on her own. Never leave her behind. The more you empower her and fuel her love, the sooner you will get there.

#Story111: Assumptions vs The Truth.

Know the difference between assumptions and the truth. Assumptions are your own (many times false) realities and the truth is actuality. Assumptions lead to expectations, which lead to disappointment, which leads to depression, broken relationships, loneliness...losing yourself and falling for whatever and whoever can catch you. Whenever you choose to assume, make sure to assume that your assumption may be wrong.

#Story112: Choices.

"Choices" is our gravity free zone, a temple with no guards where we can make decisions that could either take us closer to our truth or further away from it. Every second, we are one thought, intention, and one decision closer or further away from it all.

#Story113: Parallel roads.

Truth is Love. Love is Truth. God is Truth. Light is Truth. The only path to God is through Love. To access Truth, you must first access yourself. Everything that stands in between you and your truth is the opposite of Truth. We call it fiction, darkness, falsehood, lies, construct, matrix, or the Devil. Labels are many. Those two opposing powers co-exist and they are constantly present everywhere. All your thoughts, emotions, intentions, and actions lay the foundation for two parallel roads. One of them leads to your truth. As within, so without. As above, so below.

#Story114: The art of letting go without letting go.

There is nothing to control. Whatever you try to control, manipulate, or keep together ends up controlling and consuming you. The more you let go, the more control you gain. It's about freeing yourself from what has a grip of you, so you can freely choose to be a part of everything without belonging to anything.

#Story115: What is personal growth?

The other day I sat inside my car with my wife and we talked for about 45 min about different things and different people. Afterwards, I said to her: "Babe, I'm really proud of us. If this entire conversation was secretly filmed and broadcasted all over the world, I would not wish to modify a single thing in it." She said, "You're so right. It's pretty incredible," as she looked at me with her deep thinking eyes.

To me, this is one way to measure my personal growth. How you act and speak when nobody is watching should be pretty close, if not identical, to when you communicate and talk to the rest of the world without any fear or doubt.

#Story116: Quick fix, long-term pain.

Motivational speakers, life coaches, trainers, business coaches, I truly want to find all the right reasons to believe in your intentions. Help me believe in the goodness of your actions and their effects. I'd appreciate if you can demonstrate and display the following to your customers/followers before you ask for their trust and money:

1. How have your techniques and teachings helped you, your closest family, and people you care about?
2. What are your intentions with your offered solutions? Do you still search for your own answers while trying to help others find theirs?
3. How will other people's lives change for the better compared to before, both short-term and long-term. Why would I trust you? How can you be so sure?
4. Do you like to help others because you think they need help or because people think they need help? Is the need artificially created? Can you locate the source of that need?
5. Do you care about others or do you care about your own success? How do you know? Care and stressing others to fix something about their life with offered solutions, are two different things.

6. Would you feel comfortable answering 10 of the most personal questions to your clients/followers without any fear or need to protect your image?

7. Are you able to track down possible byproducts of your offered solutions?

#Story117: Selfies.

Statistics show that people are ready to die for a good selfie that will generate likes. Validation from others is the "cheapest" therapy disguised as an addiction that doesn't heal any wounds. I wonder if the creators of the "like" button could have imagined what psychological effects they would have on people around the world. Probably not, as they were most likely just trying to make a name for themselves while chasing greatness. That's how everything gets distorted. We create out of passion, but we rarely take the time to understand our own passions when creating and buying into solutions. We are all responsible for our own lives and we need to pay more attention to our everyday "normalized" routines and what they truly mean to us. How they enrich our lives, or how they can completely ruin us. Our selfies can serve a much greater purpose to our personal journey than a validation generator through self-presentation. Each time we share a self-image, we need to take the time for self-reflection through observation of our personal views and opinions of ourselves. Questions such as: "Why did I take this photo? What do I like about it that I so strongly believe that others may like it too? Why is it important to me to share it with the rest of the world? What do I expect to get in return and why? What if I don't get what I expected - will my self-image still be the same?"

Learning to observe our senses, emotions, needs, and desires through the essence of our higher self is
the only way for us to objectively track our personal growth. Our personal observations of ourselves are real. Observations by outsiders that are based on our presentation are false. There is a fine line between our actual and false reality.

"Being consciously aware is the new survival skill that is becoming a necessity."

#Story118: Procrastination.

Your mind is comfortable with routines and familiar patterns. It doesn't like change. Changing personal routines is a software update for your mind. During the update phase you may experience limbo, certain fear, and discomfort, but once the update is completed, you will get used to the new energy pattern and will no longer feel the need to procrastinate. It's just a mind trick. The trick is to trick your mind and not let your mind trick you.

#Story119: Farewell liquor.

Four days ago, I said goodbye to alcohol. It was sudden and unplanned. I'm not sure what happened to be completely honest. I had my first glass as I always do on a Thursday evening at our home bar. As I was sipping the liquid, I started asking myself - why do I even drink? Was this just an old habit that I haven't really looked at before? I'm not really a heavy drinker and it never interfered in my life. At least that's what I thought, until now. But now, I'm suddenly being bothered by my habit. The next day, I spent the entire day trying to find three good reasons why I should drink, but I ended up finding 25 reasons telling me that alcohol is no good for me.

Honesty, it feels so freaking good to have made this decision. Maybe it's because it came so suddenly. Maybe it's because I'm more in tune with my body and mind nowadays, or maybe because I was never brave enough to admit that I wasn't comfortable being myself all the time. I love being who I am in my new format and without any influences, whether it be substances, people, or programs. I like how this turned out.

#Story120: Hey Ladies.

Ladies, you don't have to prove that you can do everything that men can do. Don't listen to the hype and encouragement that comes from all the wrong places. Your gift is that you can do everything that men CAN'T do. That's what makes you equal and unique. Without your gifts and qualities, men (and women) would no longer exist. Fight for your right to be women and to be able to do everything that women can do. Don't let your parents tell you that they wish you were a boy. Don't let society and its agenda tell you that you can't do what men can. Those are triggers. Don't let anyone take your biggest power away from you. It's a trap. A trap that takes you further away from your truth. There is a reason you were put in this world. You can only find that reason if you fully embrace who you are and not fight for what you are not. Never forget why the force of nature is called Mother Nature!

#Story121: AI (Artificial Intelligence).

Saying that AI (Artificial Intelligence) will eventually replace us humans is like saying that light bulbs will eventually replace the Sun. Intelligence, just like the light, comes from nature (God/Higher Power/Our Source/Our Creator). Even artificial light and intelligence has nature as its source and not the other way around! Science, research, and the AI community can argue all they want but AI may only be as intelligent as the levels of the AI creators. With that said, I'm more interested in the intentions of those who push for the AI agenda, than in their capacity.

#Story122: Mind detox.

Detoxing your body with random trendy juices, teas and diets trends is great, but their effects will always be temporary if you don't take the time to detox your mind as well. Your body has natural ways of detoxing and healing itself, but those mechanisms don't work the way they should if your energy doesn't flow properly throughout your entire being. It all gets traced back to your mental and spiritual blocks that are connected to our energy vortexes (chakras) within your body. Yoga trends, food, meditation, pills, powders, workouts...all of that is just optional. But deprogramming your mind is necessary.

Detoxing (reprogramming/rebooting) one's mind is not, and never will be, a "one-size fits all" solution. Please don't buy into random solutions presented as programs that are offered out there. They can be additional layers of "infections" to your already intoxicated mind. It's not something we can do overnight. This is a journey that takes time and effort. Start slowly, gradually and simply.

Here are a few simple everyday things that can corrupt the way you think, feel, and the way you make choices in life based on distorted reality:

- Music with toxic lyrics that makes you feel like it understands you and aligns with your personal problems. It even gives you a sense of energy or an adrenaline boost.

- Politicians who want you to side with them to help them push through their agendas while criticizing opposing sides, calling them unqualified, or saying that they care more about you than "the other guys" do.
- Media that feeds your mind with emotional triggers and clickbait based news-delivery just to get your attention, so they can generate advertising revenue.
- Social Media - your feed is strategically selected and presented to you to trap you in illusionary sub-realities to make you feel like your life is less valuable and less attractive, while it completely steals your soul.
- Idolization of celebrities while falling into the trap of their agenda, their causes, their lifestyle that is presented to you. Remember that you don't get to peek behind the curtains. Be cautious, be observant. See entertainment as entertainment and nothing else.
- People you surround yourself with. Which ones give you peace and which ones create an emotional rollercoaster for you?

- Lifestyle habits that are habits and not a necessity. Start freeing yourself from them one at the time.

#Story123: People close to you don't understand you?

People close to you have limited ability to understand you beyond who they already think that you are. Once you start growing and changing, don't expect them to understand you right away. Don't talk about your progress and growth. Show it with your actions instead. Actions that affect both you and them in a positive way. They may not understand what you tell them, but they will understand what you show them.

#Story124: Question: How do you find beauty in humanity and the world around you?

Answer: The more beauty you find in yourself, the more beauty will you be able to see in others. Start looking for the good in people and everything around you, including social media, for one week. Try to ignore everything negative, bad, evil, dark, and just look for the good. This is much harder to accomplish than what it sounds, but if you find a way to complete a full week of this experiment, you have no idea what you may discover, not just around you but also inside of you. It's pretty magical actually.

#Story125: Filling that void.

I bought this beautiful car about a year and a half ago hoping it would fill a void. After the initial novelty and the adrenaline rush wore off, the car did nothing for me. I couldn't even enjoy it. It's only now, when I've come to the realization that this car meant absolutely nothing to me, that I actually enjoy driving it. I enjoy it because I wouldn't care if I didn't have it tomorrow. I'd still feel the same as if I had it. Nothing in this world should own us. We shouldn't belong to things. Things should belong to us.

#Story126: Praying for the first time.

I never knew how to pray because I never asked for anything from God, but now I wake up every day and I thank God for his mercy, for forgiving me so many times, and for always showing me the right path and for guiding me with his light.

Silent prayer, praying out loud, meditation...it doesn't matter how we choose to connect to a higher power, but one thing is for sure - we all need it sooner or later. Also, we don't always need a religion to find our way to God. It's optional and for many people, religion has been a block to connect to God. Our connection to God is intimate and personal.

#Story127: Letting God in.

We spend more time arguing, fighting, and trying to prove to each other whose God is the right one, that somewhere along the road, we lost the point of what God truly means. I strongly believe that the more we find ourselves, the more we find out who we truly are, the closer we get to God, and the more we understand his love. It doesn't even matter what religion, what you call God, or how you pray. Sometimes, it feels so good to let go of the need to super analyze and control everything, or let our thoughts take us to places where we shouldn't go. Just pray, meditate, or practice whatever ritual you like that can help you quiet your mind so you can search deeper into yourself and connect to your emotions, to your entire being, and try to become one with everything around you. Do it however many times a day you need. Whenever you feel you're off track, when you feel angry, disappointed, hopeless, depressed, anxious, or worried. That's one way to let God in, to let him meet us halfway, and to help him help us. We all need help sometimes. Help from something much greater than what we can comprehend.

> *"It doesn't even matter what religion, what you call God, or how you pray. Sometimes it feels so good to let go of the need to super analyze and control*

everything, or let our thoughts take us to places where we shouldn't go. "

#Story128: What does it mean to be a man or a woman?

Besides the traditional physical and certain surface psychological differences, what makes us a man or a woman? Is it a feeling? But how can we trust our feelings if they constantly change? Is it a hormonal thing? But how can we trust hormones if their levels are non-existent at a certain age? Is it a social thing? Should social norms define genders and what they mean? Why would we trust social norms when it has been equally corrupted and changed throughout history? So what is it? When is a gender assigned to us? Could it possibly be that sex emits a frequency unique to either sex that allows us to access our lightbody that is necessary for healing traumas, pain, and overcome original sins accordingly?

Could it be that in order for men or women to find inner peace and balance (perfect harmony) we must live according to a certain frequency as our creator originally made us? Each time we go outside of that frequency, we create havoc within us and outside of us. Each time we lose ourselves, we can always fall back and trust our Creator's plan. God doesn't make mistakes. There is a perfect order. The only disorder is the one we create in our mind.

"Besides the traditional physical and

certain surface psychological differences,
what makes us a man or a woman?"

#Story129: Men want sex, women want love.

Men want sex, but need love. Women want love, but need sex. It's an unbalanced equation. It's about the different programs that date back to the original sins. It's one of the most complex mathematical equations. I believe it is like this for a specific reason. The only way for men and women to bypass their egos that carry differences in order to have their souls merge together is through love. Men and women need to compromise in different ways through personal growth in order to achieve balance.

#Story130: The lure of lust.

Lust is not a strong sexual desire for strangers or for unknown situations, scenarios, roles, social problems, social norms involving sexual interpretation and implementation. It's about our own rooted issues that one is not able to recognize and when those imprinted memories get triggered by certain situations or people, we perceive it as an attraction. We get sexually aroused by what we perceive as certain attractive individuals, but it's actually not about them, it's about our own issues (darkness) that we are not able to recognize.

#Story131: Judging or observing?

It's a very blurred line between judging and observing, but yet there are clear differences when approaching these two. Criticizing other individuals or groups of people based on their lifestyle, way of living, race, age, and physical attributes is judging. Criticizing actions or intentions that directly or indirectly affect you or others is observing and evaluating.

"It's a very blurred line between judging and observing, but yet there are clear differences when approaching these two."

#Story132: Thank you God.

I don't know how to pray. Religion has always seemed so intimidating and scary but with you, God, I feel peaceful and I find comfort in your presence. I just wanted to take this moment and thank you God. Thank you for forgiving me so many times and for never leaving me alone. I have felt your presence and your power. Now, I also feel your mercy and that I'm a part of your plan. You always wanted nothing but love for me. I can see it now when I look back. My rebellious curiosity made me search in places and in people who couldn't give it to me. But how could they when they were equally as lost as myself? Please forgive them like you forgave me. We all want to do the right thing, but many times we don't know how. If I was able to find my way to you, all your children can do the same. We got distracted, but we need you now more than ever. Thank you for not leaving our side. I don't want to ask for anything. This love you have given to me and my family is all a man can ask for.

"I don't know how to pray.
Religion has always seemed
so intimidating and scary but
with you, God, I feel peaceful
and I find comfort in your presence."

#Story133: Getting out of my head.

I have had so many brutal "battles" with myself lately. Some of them felt like strong earthquakes. I truly felt centuries of programs, ancestral blocks and curses that I was fighting and I've gotta tell you, sometimes it got exhausting.

It's pretty crazy actually. Sometimes I wonder how I even survived. Most of those things I worked on internally are supposed to take time and many years, but I guess I've always been the type of person who likes to push the limits. I wonder often if this personal growth process is even healthy. It seems that I'm enjoying the victories, but when I think about it, it almost feels like an addiction. Can an addiction be healthy? Maybe I should slow down a bit. I think I need to get out of my mind. I just have to live as I preach, it doesn't really get more complicated than that. Our mind can truly be our biggest enemy if we are not cautious.

#Story 134: The world against you or you against the world?

It's all in your head. The feeling is rooted and it comes from somewhere. Never leave the house believing the entire world is against you. If you do, you are opening yourself up for negativity as it will be the only type of energy you'll be able to recognize; hate, anger, irritation. You'll be walking around with a chip on your shoulder. Allow yourself to think the opposite and see what happens. Let the good stuff feed into you instead. Let the light in. This is the only way to separate and to know which bad vibes are your own and which are coming from other places and people. Don't carry the weight of the entire world. Let the world carry its own weight.

It's still okay to have a bad day, but it's not okay to allow yourself to have a bad week, or a bad month, year, or a bad life. Take control over it as soon as you feel alone in this world and as soon as you feel that everybody is against you. The world loves you because you were put here for a reason - don't forget that. But you need to be open for that love. It will come from places you don't expect.

> *"Never leave the house*
> *believing the entire*
> *world is against you."*

#Story135: Everyone is right for what they know.

Most of us wish to comprehend the world we live in, and many of us construct our own personal theories to help us make sense of daily life. Many branches of today's society provide easy explanations of our surroundings and even definitions of our own inner self. The majority of people content themselves with whatever degree of understanding they have managed to achieve about their existence. Some initiate the search when they stumble upon difficulties or experience a very low satisfaction level of happiness, despite the amount of external success they achieve. No matter how much I search, one thing seems to be for sure - that everyone is right for the level of knowledge they have. Realizing this has given me such wonderful peace and harmony when talking to others. I no longer try to convince anyone to adopt my opinions and perspectives. I simply embrace theirs and use them as a reference for my own knowledge and understanding.

"No matter how much I search, one thing seems to be for sure - that everyone is right for the level of knowledge they have. Realizing this has given me such wonderful peace and harmony when talking to others."

#Story136: Introspection, extrospection, general perception.

I have a simplified and shortened "do-it-myself" method for those who wish to initiate self-exploration of one's own world. It consists of:

Introspection, also known as human self-reflection. It is the examination or observation of one's own mental and emotional processes and the desire to learn more about their fundamental nature, behavior, purpose, and essence.

Extrospection is the observation of all things external to one's own mind. Extrospection is the ordinary sense perception or reasoning concerning things, people, situations, that are perceived.

General Perception is how the world perceives you. General Perception of the rest of the world when it comes to you is a great way to compare your own discoveries about yourself with how the world perceives you. Most people accept that other people's perception of them does matter. Others think that what other people think of them is of no importance at all. These people are right to some extent. However, they're risking putting themselves in the same category as those who care too much about the general perception. These people tend to be what one would describe as 'thick skinned' and they are not bothered about what other people think of them.

It's a seamless combination of these three that carries our balance, and the truth is somewhere in between all of them.

#Story137: You are more than what it appears to be.

You are not your emotions, thoughts, beliefs, desires, or senses. We are not even our happiness, our mindset, our goals, or our ego. There is a higher essence in us; a higher self that observes and oversees our life journey. Once we find the key to the door where the truth about us resides, we become masters of our destiny. It's the secret to feeling motivated and full of life even when not getting any credit, recognition or validation for what you are doing or what you have. That is where your true strength resides - you being able to let go of all the things that you believe is giving you control, but are, in fact controlling you.

That is when difficulties become possibilities through your ability to redefine your goals and transform yourself into something broader and greater than it appears to be.

#Story138: You are not your parents.

Love your parents and appreciate what they have done for you, but you still need to face traumas, wounds, and darkness that their behavior may have caused you. Many times, this is unintentional and without their awareness. It's simply passed down from generation to generation. The cycle must be broken in order to heal.

#Story139: It's ok to be unhappy.

People's concept of happiness consists of ideas that other people have predefined. If you feel unhappy, start looking at what you have adopted as your own concept of happiness and if ask yourself whether that needs any modification to suit your own life. Being happy on your own terms without other attachments and definitions is the goal in this whole equation. Being temporarily unhappy is just a phase and not your life.

"People's concept of happiness consists of ideas that other people have predefined."

#Story140: The perfect business deal.

The secret to a good business deal is having all parties walk away feeling like winners. What you put out there in the universe will always come back to visit you sooner or later.

#Story141: Know your circle of people and their priorities.

It's truly about priorities in life. Family are people who you consider to be your first circle of people in the priority diagram depending on where you are in your life journey:
1. People that heal you.
2. People that you need healing from.
3. People you work with.
4. People who you meet in daily life.
5. People that you heal.

You can't water all your relationships at once. Focus on the circle of people that you need the most at different phases of your life. That way, you don't let anyone become an energy vampire.

#Story142: Universal love and romantic love are not the same.

I've come to the realization that we need to redefine and separate the confusion and meaning behind universal love and romantic love. It's clearly creating a lot of pain in people who believe that they must be married or find their soulmate in order to feel loved. It's far from the truth. Everyone is loved and filled with universal love, but many are blocked from accessing it due to social programming, conditioning, media, pressure, and expectations. Romantic love is optional. We somehow came to believe that we must depend on other people in order to be loved and feel loved. That's exactly the opposite. We are not able to feel love or give love unless we are filled with the universal love. We search for love in other people, but what we actually seek is someone to help us heal and fill that void. Godly love is the love you carry within yourself. That's the universal love and light that we should always consciously try to fill ourselves with.

"I've come to the realization that we need to redefine and separate the confusion and meaning behind universal love and romantic love."

#Story143: There is nowhere to go.

Shoot for the stars, move to a different location, change jobs, change friends, change partners, change clothes, change style, change cars, take escape drugs and alcohol. I'm afraid there is nowhere to go. Sometimes, all we need to do is to change our thoughts and perception, escape our own negativity, and shoot for the higher self.

#Story144: Reality Escapes...

I wanted to make a toast to another "real" story about our "unreal" desires for finding new ways of escaping our "reality" that we work so hard for. There is no effective way of escaping reality. Nobody has ever succeeded and documented it. There are temporary illusions of escape that can make us feel different. That is completely okay if we are aware of what that escape truly means while we keep one goal in mind - to fix our real reality so we no longer need to escape from it. The tricky part is locating coordinates showing us how far is too far. For those losing sight of the shore on the boat of life, it can be a stormy experience of no return.

#Story145: The boy and the gentleman.

I've learned when it's okay to let the boy in me come forward and act out and have fun. The gentleman that I'm becoming needs the boy in me who fearlessly dreamed about becoming the man I am today. I give him access to all of the things he once wanted so badly. It's still important to the boy in me to let it all out once in a while. But I'm cautious nowadays and I'm making sure to treat the boy as a boy should be treated. He needs someone to look up to, he needs guidance, he needs a role model, he needs to know when it's time to stop the fun and go back to being a gentleman again.

I'm not ready nor do have the need to let other people and their judgments, social pressure, and responsibilities take the fun out of me. I signed up for growing up, but I didn't sign up for stopping having fun.

"I signed up for growing up but I never signed up for stopping having fun."

#Story146: I can't compromise on being me.

My peace with my inner equilibrium is my priority nowadays. I can no longer allow my surface self to dictate my image or my social life. I like to build meaningful friendships and relationships based on depth and honesty. I like having relationships where both sides understand the importance of being there for each other the right way without the fear of offending one another. Platonic emotions that lead to immature behaviors no longer have a place in an environment where awareness is the master and ignorance is the servant.

"Every morning I wake up with one main goal; to have evolved from yesterday. It doesn't matter in what way - spiritual, mental, physical, intellectual. There actually isn't any other way. Going towards the center is the only way up."

#Story147: Take care of your body, not someone else's agenda.

Seeing constant reminders on TV, social media, advice from friends and colleagues, advertisement, gyms, the diet and fashion industry - these things all stress you to be summer or beach body ready, and can create anxiety, pressure, and a sense of inadequacy.

Chances are those people are not aware of the agendas they belong to. Let them do their thing, but you don't have to fall into that trap. If someone believes that achieving a certain body type, gaining or losing a few pounds, or getting a two, four, six, eight, or whatever pack will give you some sort of fulfillment, joy, and happiness or be the only way to enjoy summer, they are obviously missing the point of life. At least for the summer. I've never met anyone who has achieved that state of mind regardless of how amazing a body they may have. It's nothing else but another search for validation from other people with methods that always let your expectations down. Do not fall into that trap, like ever. Do not let anyone have power over you with their own manifestation of insecurities that lead to emotional destruction. If you breathe, you are summer ready, simple as that. Enjoy every second of your life just the way you are. Enjoying the here and now will only add value and joy to your journey to whatever that journey may be.

#Story148: How to connect to other people.

When you meet people, don't try to find flaws in them. Try to find the good in them. When you speak to them, speak to their best side - don't speak to the devil in them, speak to the angel in them. It will leave you both feeling more empowered. Relationships with others start with yourself. It's hard to properly connect to other people or establish deep meaningful relationships that add value to your life and not take away from it without your ability to connect to your true self first. The more you have a shallow connection to yourself, the more shallow relationships you will build with others. You may experience nothing but disappointments, rejection, betrayal, and a constant need for company and loudness. It's a very destructive approach that leaves trails of emptiness in you regardless of how many people you may surround yourself with. Master solitude while letting other people in with personal boundaries and honesty.

"In order for you to get to see the true colors of everyone, you must first be able to see through all the shades of yourself."

#Story149: Can you trust your intentions?

For one to be defined, the opposite must also be defined. Darkness has brightness, all has nothing, good has bad, life has death, cold has heat, yin has yang, left has right, up has down, love has hate...The difference between the opposites is often the way we present and perceive the truth. Fire can either burn you or warm you. Guns can either protect or create destruction. But it all starts with your intentions and your intentions can never be trusted until you fully know yourself, including your darkness, your light, your ego, your wants, your needs, your passions, and your triggers.

#Story150: Protect your mind.

The books you read, the movies and TV shows you watch, the music that you listen to, the people you surround yourself with, the people you meet, the advertising you fall for, the peer pressure you can't resist, the career you chase, conversations you engage with, things you react to, and the agendas you belong to. Check the list above and see if you discover something that doesn't serve your journey.

#Story151: The people I meet lately.

The types of people I've been connecting with lately:

1. People that are self-aware, deep, but functional. People that can stimulate me either mentally, spiritually, intellectually.
2. People that I can stimulate the same way, as mentioned above, and as I observe how they channel that energy and knowledge, I learn from their actions and reactions.

#Story152: It's a perfect order.

When looking at people around me both on social media and in real life, so many are acting like the world is upside down. Everyone is offering solutions and suggestions for something better or something that could lead to something more significant than what the world currently has. I'm just curious why nobody wonders if things are exactly the way they are supposed to be at the moment. Maybe everything is great and no adjustments are needed? In order to suggest changes or to make things better, don't we need to know where we are headed? Are we just running forward or even worse, in circles without a clue what exactly we are looking for?

"When looking at people around me both on social media and in real life, so many are acting like the world is upside down."

#Story153: No hesitation, only love.

I asked her to jump with me into the unknown. I wasn't looking for an answer; I was looking for doubt and certitude. There was no right or wrong answer, only the truth where nothing means everything and everything means nothing; where everything remains the same, but nothing will ever be like it was before regardless of the answer; where everything sounds confusing but nothing is as clear...You are a one of a kind woman Cat. I love you.

#Story154: Frustration.

I can feel how my frustration is slowly fading away. It still makes some sound, but I can bear it. Wow, now when I think about it, frustration is nothing else but the lower dimensions sensing that something more clear was vibrating one or a few levels up. I just wanted to be heard the way I knew I could be heard, and the way I wanted to be heard. I got frustrated when some did not listen, but now I realize that it was me and not them. I just had some additional climbing to do. Incredible and magical.

#Story155: Touching your souls with my words.

Throughout this journey, I've talked to so many strangers that I have never met and don't even know what they look like, but our souls have connected through each word we type. It's incredible, as it feels like I've always known them. Like old souls that have wandered around for lifetimes. It made me wonder why this rarely happens in "real life." What is stopping us? Can our surface and presentation truly be so much in our way? Maybe we never tried to let our guard down and give it a try. Let me try to bypass my own layers of filters and let me see if I can connect with souls in real life the same way I do through my social media. There must be a way. I know that there is a way.

"It's incredible, as it feels
like I've always known them.
Like old souls that have
wandered around for lifetimes."

#Story156: Loving yourself vs loving yourself.

Make sure you understand the difference between loving yourself as a human being and loving yourself as an identity. What your ego is trying to do is create in your mind and manifest out there in the physical world. If you realize the difference you will solve all your pain. Your self-love should NEVER be related to the constructs in your head!

"If you're interested in the true meaning of something, you must search for it. If you're interested in an answer, you may Google it."

#Story157: Internet bullies.

When those comments and messages trigger you, never, ever believe what people say about you. That's their own subconscious reality seeking ways to justify their emotional, spiritual and mental state through projection, while spreading its negativity and homogenizing the environment. When people judge you, all you need to know that they are speaking about themselves. There is something going on in their mind that has nothing to do with you. Use it a chance to find out why it bothers you.

"When people judge you, all you need to know that they are speaking about themselves."

#Story158: You're not obliged to:

Answer people's texts right away or ever. Send holiday or birthday cards. Talk to strangers in elevators. Agree or nod when someone talks to you just to be polite. Show up to an event only because you feel an obligation, but you know you will be miserable. Be politically correct out of fear of being judged. Smile when you don't feel like smiling. To say thanks to people for things you didn't ask for. Let people pressure you to do things, to be a certain way, or to go with an agenda that doesn't align with your personal needs for the moment.

Do something because you truly want to, not because you feel obliged. Try it and see what you discover.

"The ultimate destination here on earth
is not a physical attainment, whether it
be a luxury or personal aesthetics.
The destination is something else.
It's reaching a level of
personal growth that you no longer
are driven by desires but by love."

#Story159: Fall for love, not for pressure.

When we agree to things or are pressured into things by other people, even when it doesn't feel 100% right, we reach a personal progressional culmination. When we no longer dare to question our personal choices, gut feelings, or needs, we limit our intellectual and spiritual ability to expand its horizons. Our individual growth ends and we fall victim to other people's agendas and needs. Dare to say no, to say yes, to be quiet, or to speak whenever it feels right even if it's wrong.

#Story160: Can you tell the difference?

Does your career belong to you or do you belong to your career?

Do you chase freedom or do you enslave yourself with the very same path that is supposed to give you freedom?

Do you learn new things or do you guard what you already know by pushing away new knowledge with stubbornness, pride, and ignorance?

Do you love unconditionally or do you try to trap others into your life to serve your needs, your checklists, and your agendas that you may not even know about?

Do people in your life give you good energy and light or do they drain your last drop of positivity leaving you empty without their or your awareness?

Do you feel pressure because there is pressure or because you created it in your head?

Do you get disappointed at people when they let you down because you had expectations from them or do you feel disappointed because you were not aware of your expectations and pressure you put on them?

Do you search for yourself (on the outside) or do you search for solutions and people that will help you escape from your pain and your problems?

Can you tell the difference?

#Story161: Expectations colliding with boundaries.

When people present themselves to you, full of expectations that comes packaged as pressure, serving agendas, and plans they have created in their own mind, it has nothing to do with you. But, expect an eruption when their expectations collide with your boundaries. You know what, that's alright. Recognize it and let them pass through. There are only so many people you can allow to stay with you, when there is renovation going on in your home.

#Story162: Phases of temptation.

I've fallen for temptation without the ability to recognize it. I've tried to avoid it, suppress it, and channel it. I've also tried facing it, bringing it close to me while being comfortable around it. It's only in the last phase that it no longer had power over me. When it started losing power over me, that's when I started seeing things for what they are and not for what they presented to be. What was chasing me, started running away from me.

"What was chasing me,
started running away
from me."

#Story163: Recognize love.

When it comes to love there is no such a thing as confused love, half love, maybe love, back and forth love. It's Love or No Love. Simple as that. Do not confuse sexual attraction, admiration for someone, or you liking the idea of someone or who that person may become. When you find it, you become it, you love it, you breath it, you don't even know how to question it, you find no ways of doubting it. You simply just become all of it and you will only know it as Love. Love, and nothing else.

#Story164: Not my other half.

I've never seen you as my other half. You've never been half a person to me. You are so complete my love. You complete me and together we are one. We have always been strong alone and as individuals, but together we are each other partner, lovers, healers. Together, we build our life out of love and not out of need. We catch each other when we fall and carry each other during our weaker moments. No halves do that. You're my other whole.

#Story165: Soulmate.

In order for your soulmate to find your soul, you need to get rid of some of those layers of hurt and pain that are acting as thick walls between you and your soul, and not letting the beauty of your soul to shine through. Even if your soulmate is in the same room, God won't let either of you look at each other until those walls are torn down...

A Soulmate is not someone who thinks and feels the same as you. They are not someone who is one with you for the sake of comfort. A soulmate is someone who completes you in all the ways that you are not.

#Story166: Recognize the real woman.

Women's love is the most mighty healing force in the world. It's our gateway, our passage and the key to the source of everything that causes us pain, but we are the only ones who can make it all go away by feeding into that love. The more fuel we give her to make her love stronger for us, the faster and the closer we get to the epicenter of our own internal strength. That's where we can make the shift of our internal powers. That's where we can turn off the pain, the darkness, our deepest nightmares, and everything that we feel is wrong about us.

Once the love is so strong that you completely heal, you may experience this release of bright energy that is perceived as positivity, understanding and unconditional love, not just for people that are close to you, but even for people that can't do anything for you. If you don't already have that woman in front of you, I'd recommend you open all your senses so when the day comes that you meet that woman, you'd will be very selective with how you treat her, how you love her, how you listen to her, how you make her feel and how you react and care when you don't make her feel the way she should. That woman can be your key to becoming the person you always wanted to become, but she will not be able to do it on her own. Never leave her behind. The more you empower her and fuel her love, the sooner you will get there.

#Story167: Creating distance.

Nowadays, the hardest thing to overcome as a couple is not that two people fall out of love, as many people believe is the case, it's because of one single word: distance! It's always minor things that potentially creates a snowball effect and becomes disastrous for relationships and marriages. A lot of couples are creating distance between each other and many don't know how to find their way back to each other. Yes, even in our "holy" relationship (as seen on IG) we too have experienced distance at some point without even noticing it. So how did we deal with it?

Although it's only one problem, I'd like to break it down into three phases:

Phase 1: Identifying and admitting that something was causing distance between us, even though our love was as strong as ever. It was almost impossible to notice and it created a huge frustration in our marriage. It was like a hypnotic state, almost borderline to despair.

Phase 2: Coming to the realization that nothing else is more important than our marriage and our love. We then started implementing all the necessary changes, one at a time, and eliminated all the repercussions of modern life that were coming in between us and creating distance. It was necessary to take the time to recognize all the hidden things that were creating distance.

Phase 3: Restructuring our lives after the rebirth of our love.

It's about going the distance and not creating it.

#Story168: Kings vs. Priests.

It seems that everyone wants to be a king nowadays. I'm afraid that a kingdom without a priesthood is an empty shell. I wish I knew this in my early twenties when the hunger to build my own empire was equal to a starving wolf. It was not until my mid-thirties that I've come to a realization that I completely missed growing the spiritual part of me. We simply cannot enjoy anything we create in this world regardless of how great our accomplishments may be unless it's balanced with divine wisdom and harmony.

#Story169: Reclaim the power over yourself.

Tips on how to empower other people to have power over you:

1. Instead of setting boundaries, feel resentful, and hold a grudge when someone takes up your time, energy and makes you feel hurt.
2. Your day totally depends on how other people behave.
3. You change your goals on a weekly or even daily basis based on what other people that don't matter in your life tell you what you should do with your life.
4. You strongly believe that the e-book you just downloaded from iTunes will change your life because the ghostwriter of that book is a great friend with the author who made millions by convincing his dad that he would quit recreational drugs once he becomes a millionaire.
5. You complain daily about all the things you "have to" do in your life.
6. You quit your job because it feels really good to hit "send" once you've passionately put together that amazing resignation letter.
7. You complain about your relationship to every friend willing to listen, but you have no plans on breaking up. Instead,

you end up blaming your friends for bad advice.

8. You always have a great business idea and feel that everyone is looking to steal it from you if they don't give you the feedback you expected.

9. You only surround yourself with people who compliment you all the time, who think you do everything right, that you're the smartest person in the room, and who do not desire to challenge your views, behavior, and life decisions with constructive criticism.

10. You think everyone on Instagram has a better life than you and you constantly Google ways to become a quick success.

11. Your feelings are deeply hurt if people leave you on "read" and only text back hours or days after.

#Story170: Presentation vs reality.

Why is it so important to us to live our lives according to social and egocentric definitions while trying to make it all look beautiful on the outside? It might look beautiful to everyone we are trying to impress, but on the inside you're an emotional mess or headed there without even knowing. You keep telling yourself to "keep going, don't stop, never give up" even if halfway through life, deep down you know that something is not right. But, you just keep going because your life looks "normal" on the outside and it looks just like everyone else's or better, so you discredit your emotional state and you continue the journey without any clarity to where or why you are headed there. Luckily, life catches up sooner or later and we are forced to act. It hits us suddenly and it gets delivered to us as a lack of ambition, motivation, absence of joy, depression, blurred vision in your journey, anxiety, toxic and unhealthy relationships. Presentation is important, I won't try to take anything away from it, but let's pause for a moment and re-evaluate how we feel and how we are doing. Let's try to be as fearless about taking care of our inner world as we are fearless about taking care of our outer world. One step at a time, one change at a time.

#Story171: Changing direction is not giving up.

Goals that no longer serve your happiness should no longer be goals. They should be archived as old plans. Only because you like the idea of something, or because you temporarily wanted it for whatever reason, it simply does not mean that you should devote more of your life to it, if it doesn't feel right. Many motivational speakers and the Internet say that "you should live here and now" but they also say "you need to focus on your goals." So which is it then? Live here and now or stress about an outcome that may not turn out as we imagined? Something is greatly missing in this equation.

Am I saying that we should all stop everything and have no goals in life? Absolutely not. Not even close. I am just showing you the possibility of how unaware our subjective self-identity can be. It can limit your options in life. I'm shedding light on other dimensions and levels of your identity so you no longer exclusively limit your life or your choices, and narrow your chances of finding fulfillment by sticking stubbornly to certain goals. Staying loyal to your goals strictly out of fear that you may disappoint yourself or betray a promise to yourself, is not a good reason to continue along a path of unhappiness.

"Staying loyal to your goals strictly out of fear that you may disappoint yourself

*or betray a promise to yourself
is not an excuse to be on a path
of unhappiness. "*

#Story172: Idolization.

Our egos are programmed to believe that anything is possible as long as there is another person who has accomplished it. Someone to look up to. A celebrity or anyone who's trained to portray and sell an illusion of what the perfect life can be, as long as we put in the work and all the other ingredients as instructed by those who sell the illusion. If you don't want to go that route and put in all that work, no worries, they can let you sample the good life through merchandise, ticket sales, and autographed nonsense that make you feel that your life is less valuable or lived in a less interesting way. This is one of the greatest ways to bypass yourself and your own happiness while falling into the trap of agendas that belong to entertainment, fashion, sports, religion, and science. Utilize them but don't belong to any of them.

#Story173: Separation of the child.

We place a pacifier in our child's mouth and feed them with plastic instead of parenting love. The moment we do that, we are making our children more open for manipulation of thoughts. An open source receptive for anything else but human love and connection. We go to work to make money, so we can pay a nanny to watch our children. The next thing you know they are grownups and we wonder why the connection between our children and us is so bad. Maybe it's because we unintentionally separated them from us with that pacifier, then it continued with childcare providers, teachers, society, friends, and media. It's not easy for parents. I too have fallen for all the above tricks, but I've learned. That's what we do. We learn. Let's be cautious and observant.

#Story174: The rise of man...

There were Dark ages, then came the Renaissance and the Enlightenment era followed by the Industrial Revolution. Landing on the moon was pretty cool too but not as cool as the tech and social media era...Throughout humanity we went on a pretty sweet roller-coaster ride in search of answers about who we are, why we are, and where we are going. We got a lot of cool answers and definitions. A few times we almost got it all figured out and just when we were about to see what's up, curtains got pulled in front of our eyes and it all became an even bigger confusion. Now, we are here sitting with all of those accomplishments and discoveries but we are still confused as ever before.

But humans are incredible, and regardless of how hopeless things may look, we always find a way to make it work. That's what we do. We fuck up a lot but that's what makes us humans and not robots. Our never ending desire to search for answers about who we are is what keeps us going forward. Let's just not forget to take a break and just enjoy the here and now and be content with the answers that we already have. Who cares and why do we need to know everything? Sometimes, we have to trust that things are exactly the way they are supposed to be and that we learn to find beauty in just existing and being in the moment.

*"There were Dark ages, then
came the Renaissance
and the Enlightenment
era followed by the Industrial
Revolution. Landing on the
moon was pretty cool too
but not as cool as the tech and
social media era..."*

#Story175: First things first.

Not everyone cares about spiritual awakening or figuring out what fulfillment, happiness, or purpose is. Some people just try to find a way to survive till the next day, despite access to all the riches and things that we thought would give us everything we dreamed about. Let's not forget about them. Let's not forget about the sick and the weak ones. Let's not forget about the hungry and homeless. Awakening is about being woke enough to realize that we need this world, but the world needs us as well. Let's do what we can, when we can and let's help who we can.

#Story176: To believe or not to believe?

The knowledge (information) that you acquire daily through third party sources is based on you putting your trust in the source completely. The only difference is the perceived legitimacy of the source. For example, you probably believe that dinosaurs once existed and that we have landed on the moon. You probably also believe that we have evolved from monkeys. You believe all of this because a governing body said so and someone decided for you that it's the truth and the information was then instilled in us. Now, I'm not saying that any of that is not true, but I can also say that it's completely false and you wouldn't be able to prove me wrong. You can argue all you want and try to gather evidence, but you weren't there when any of the events occurred. Some may even get upset as their so called knowledge is being questioned and their ego is doing everything it can to protect it.

When you buy health products, there are thousands of brands that make identical claims about their products being the gold standard and the absolute best on the market. They make all of those claims completely legally and nobody can prove them wrong or right because so many circumstances and relative factors are involved. My point is, when you walk through life, what you do is to settle for information, experiences, and your reality that is mostly created based on someone else's truth and discoveries and not on your own. That is okay, and you are allowed to live like that, but it also removes your authority to make absolute claims and judgmental opinions about other people's opinions, way of living, and their choices or beliefs. Accepting everyone and their way of living is your number one step to accepting yourself.

#Story177: Going out.

Going out used to be fun but unfulfilling, without ever knowing why. At this stage of my life, there is nothing for me out there after 10 p.m. The pull to go out and search for something all night has been cut to its roots. But who knows, maybe I'm just getting older and love the idea of going to bed at 10 p.m., and waking up at 6 a.m. to do my morning workout. Either way, I like this new discovery and this new routine.

#Story178: Finding yourself without destroying yourself.

Start by observing and evaluating your emotions, reactions, feelings, guilt, expectations, frustrations, and every other signal your inner self is sending you when you interact with other people. Then you need to track what causes that specific feeling. If it's repetitive, it only means something is off. You need to learn how to say no to things and people when something doesn't feel right without the fear of losing friends, social status or control of something that makes no sense. In other words, you need to be prepared to temporarily let go a big portion of everything and everyone around you that could be a shield between you and your truth. Layer by layer, heavy bag after heavy bag, needs to go until you reach a balance. No hesitant or sudden changes. Growth is and should be as seamless as possible without disruption of your everyday life.

#Story179: Normalized addiction.

What is an addiction? I would say it's a repetitive torture of your body, mind, and soul with different substances, behavior, patterns, people, and habits. But how often is it okay according to social norms? If you go out every weekend and drink it's considered "normal" and okay by the general public. If you do it every day, you'll be considered an addict. But isn't every weekend a repetitive cycle? A pattern that you belong to? So why isn't that considered an addiction? Because so many have adopted it? What about the thriving coffee industry? Have you ever seen a coffeehouse franchise going out of business? The caffeine injection is served to you in different flavors, temperatures, and locations but you don't question what it actually does to your overall well-being, your mind, and your soul. Your body doesn't even get to recover before it gets injected with another dose of caffeine. That's not addiction? Only when you beat the normalized addictions, will you be able to recognize other hidden addictions in yourself.

#Story180: A few simple questions.

It's not possible to see through the pretense of the world, or understand humanity without first understanding ourselves. No matter how much we try to get a grip of the world around us, it will always be our own projections we see. It all starts with simple questions. Why do you feel frustrated over things you have no control over? Why do you feel jealousy and fear of losing someone when you know that the person loves you and only wants you? Why are you afraid to share your most intimate sexual desires with the person you say you love the most? Why do you feel that you always let people down when the only person that thinks that is you? Why do you need to feel liked, loved and wanted by people that don't matter to you? Why do you feel betrayed when people don't do as you expected? Why do politicians trigger the worst in you when you have never even met them in real life? Ask yourself those questions, but make sure to not let your ego answer for you. Don't expect to find answers right away. Look for answers when real life scenarios occur. You may be surprised what you find out.

#Story181: Perception can fool you.

Your mind is a receiver; your senses collect information around you. The information has to bypass several filters and layers such as emotions, wounds, acquired knowledge both true and untrue, and prejudices until it reaches your brain where your perception is shaped. The more filters and layers information has to bypass, the more distorted everything you perceive will be.

Ever wonder why people prefer to see things for what they are presented as, instead for what they truly are? It's because most of the time, they have no ability to see through it. They fall for the presentation.

#Story182: You are not perfect.

Everyone wants to make a change. The first mistake people make is to cut off other people, quit their job, or go to a different city. In some drastic cases, this may be necessary, but in most cases it's starting at the wrong end of the spectrum to initiate your change. It's extremely important to check yourself weekly or preferably daily. You have to ask yourself if you may be that person who has negative energy, who is always critical of others, always finds something and someone to complain about, always victimizes yourself, holds grudges and feels hurt for every little thing, pushing away people, or holding on to them for your own needs and agendas. If you're honest with yourself and find a pattern in any of the behaviors above, then you need to stay exactly where you are, keep everything the way it is, and initiate your change while using your current life as a measurement for your progress. Any new environment or people would not do you any justice as it may take years to develop new honest relationships that would be helpful in a real way.

#Story183: Freedom & success.

Today's definition of freedom and success is being able to find meaning, joy, and fulfillment in everything that we do in life, even small tasks, without feeling a pull from a different direction. A pull manifested as an unsettled feeling. Just being able to be present and feel fulfilled by life itself without additional needs or attachments is freedom. Reaching a level of personal growth where we can separate attachments, riches, and other energy pulls as optional experiences in life and not as necessities to feel happiness. That is the truest freedom there is.

#Story184: Question: When did you start your search?

Answer: it's been a slow process since I can remember. Always some sort of search without knowing what I was searching for. The last two years have been intense, especially after I started getting out of the fitness industry. Everything I was doing at the time seemed to be so meaningless, so I just let it all go. Now, I realized that I was slowly healing my rooted issues and the things that I was doing in my life that were originated from my rooted passions were no longer serving any purpose. I didn't realize at the time what it was and why I was feeling unfulfilled by things that always given me a sense of joy and belonging. It was a "blind" search at the time.

Then the search started becoming more intense. I just had to figure out my own shit and as I was doing it, I was getting more clear and aware. For each issue I solved, I got to "see more." As I was seeing more, I also saw more pain and suffering in others as well. It turns out that most people shared the same pain. I started sharing my thoughts through social media and many seemed to find help and comfort in my writing. My followers insisted that I write a book, so I decided to do so. I had so much to write about. As I was writing my stories I started discovering more things I personally needed to fix. Here I am now. 10,000 some stories narrowed down to 369 stories.

#Story185: Meatless Sundays.

I've decided to make each Sunday a meat free day. It feels so light and good to give my body and mind a break from instinct driven eating. Maybe I'll never become a vegetarian, I haven't decided yet, but I'm sure that I can devote one day a week and turn to other sources of protein than meat, chicken, and even fish. Let's see what that does for me.

#Story186: Money, power(less).

The main source of our unfulfillment is our never ending desire and search for power, money, things, validation, followers, friends & lovers without ever asking where the need comes from. All those desires are disguised as a search for happiness, love, and purpose while trying to fill a void. It's stubbornness that makes us refuse to confront ourselves and our darkness that leaves us feeling empty, angry, lonely, unfulfilled and more powerless than ever before. And so it continues, generations after generations until someone breaks the cycle. Why can't that someone be you, me, her, him, them?

#Story187: Wisdom through Ego.

I don't want to make it sound like I'm giving the Ego a bad name. It may come across that way, but I want to point out that an egoless existence is not possible. At least not in my world. I've tried to go as far as I can in order to see what can be removed and what can be left of the ego while trying to be functional.

Outgrowing the ego does not mean waging a war against the ego. If we do start a war against our ego, it only means that our sub-ego takes over. Sub-ego is your spiritual ego. Outgrowing the ego means that we mature and we slowly move to a higher context of self and we no longer identify with our own limitations - titles, things we have, or knowledge we have acquired. We no longer react to nonsense but rather, we *act* when we recognize nonsense and try to turn it into sense. Ego is still the driving force, the engine of it all, but transcending it means that it runs on more purified energy.

#Story188: Think. Feel. Believe.

Our sometimes infinite struggle consists of balancing the truth that is stuck somewhere in between our thinking, feeling, and believing. Do we think, do we feel, or do we believe? Maybe the outcome is the value of all three variables combined making a balanced trinity? Our truth can't be anything else but the balance of independent, dependent, and controlled energy that circulates in perfect harmony in order to help us come to clarity when making any decisions that can lead to changes in our personal journey.

#Story189: Being egocentric is a phase.

Being egocentric can potentially be damaging, that is correct, but many of us have to go through a phase of our lives where we are highly self-centered. Those phases are related to our early life and rooted issues. Egocentrism is a healing process, a way for many to find love for themselves and fill a void. That's why we always need to look for the good in people and not focus on their egocentric side and the temporary identity they have created. Every person has another much brighter side and the more we speak to that side, the more beauty we may find in every individual. Try to see beyond the facade.

#Story190: Rowing together.

If everything is connected, then what part of our existence is personal? Why are we so harsh towards ourselves when we fail at certain things in life? We didn't set the rules, after all, and so many circumstances and variables are constantly changing and completely out of our control so why do we get offended for things we are not responsible for. Why do we feel insulted if everything other people say are just pure projections? Maybe there are some shared responsibilities in the whole picture? If everything is connected and nothing is personal than why all the rush, stress, hurt, blame, guilt, anger? We are in it together. We are rowing together in the same boat.

#Story191: Does money give you power?

Money without elevated awareness and self-conquest controls people and their free will. I see money as a test in life. A test to win over greed. If all basic needs are covered, and a person still blindly chases money without the ability to separate himself from it, then he belongs to it. Money is one of the strongest energy patterns that acts as a blindfold on our soul if we are not cautious. There's nothing wrong about making money, but blindly chasing money is greed and getting out of that maze is one of life's hardest challenges. Before the battle against greed is won, I'm afraid it's difficult to climb higher. It's a filter, a barrier, and a test.

#Story192: Question: Is reality and this life a big test?

We were given consciousness and free will for a reason. Our existence is important. It's important to not see life as a starting and an ending point but rather as an infinite cycle. We are tested daily and it's our choices, actions, and intentions that either take us closer or further away from the divine power. God doesn't want us to fail, God created us out of love and God wants us to succeed in this life. We just have to start opening our eyes and start redefining our priorities and the definition of success, test, failure, happiness, truth, love, life, and existence.

#Story193: Is humility a virtue?

Having a modest, humble or low view of one's own importance is a new-age social program presented as a virtue that is not really necessary if we stick to the 7 fundamental virtues. Humility is a distorted addition to the 7 fundamental virtues that have already been defined for more than 2,500 years within both the philosophical and theological concept. They are equally relevant and accurate today as they were 2,500 years ago. Those virtues are prudence, temperance, justice, courage, faith, hope, and charity. We attain those by finding a way to restrain and channel our biologically driven emotional states such as lust, anger, jealousy, greed, gluttony that all date back to the original "sins." Lust and greed specifically are the biggest "animals" that we all must face at one point in our lives in order to be able to even recognize virtues in its authentic shape and not just through theories, teachings, or programmed words. Virtues are more than just words. They are as real as our existence.

"Making time for greatness is voluntary.
Making time for sadness is mandatory."

#Story194: Victim of pressure: A message from my wife.

"I just feel that there has been so much pressure and control placed on women making us create our own prison of suffering and stress in the name of "success" or "doing it all." I was such a victim of it too. All of that was just a block keeping me from being able to find true joy and peace. I'm so thankful to be able to live life now so fully, peacefully and "in color" as I like to say, and to truly enjoy every moment with you and Layla."

#Story195: Growth: A message from a follower.

"Gosh this is so deep! Sometimes I feel like I've really come a long way in overcoming my old programs, I react less, I judge less, I need less, I observe more...but sometimes I feel like a baby that needs to be spoon fed purées and yet can't understand a thing, so somehow I wish you could explain in detail what you mean with certain posts, comments, etc. and it's only then that I realized the depth of your teachings because truth will only be discovered by those who truly seek. Otherwise, we will be allowing another program in blind faith. Thank you for guiding us on this journey."
- An Instagram Follower

#Story196: Love or parenting? A message exchange with a follower.

Q: I want to ask how you raise your daughter other than showing love. What do you do to teach her the things you never learn in schools and etc?

Me: Love.

Q: But just love cannot help you get through this life. People will let you down and some people don't appreciate the love you give them.

Me: I believe you misunderstand love. Love carries truth. Truth carries everything we need to know and access in this life, including instructions on how to handle the issues that you're mentioning. Let's not romanticize love. It's the most powerful force and the most profound wisdom known in our existence.

#Story197: You-Niversal Patterns.

The more I search, the more I see patterns that lead to one and only universal truth. Somehow our personal subjective reality seems to be structured around it as we all struggle to prove to each other who's more right.

Truthfully, all I see are different layers of awareness, but all patterns lead to the same master programs and ultimately the same truth so what are we all fighting about? There is absolutely nothing but our own illusions that are stopping us from accomplishing peace and love among us. Why is everyone mad? Let's calm the beast, so we can see the light.

#Story198: Guilt.

Guilt is an extension of the Obedience program. It can resurface in our life in different ways. For example, when someone puts pressure on you to do something against your will, guilt may trick you to believe that you are wrong and that you must go ahead and do what you're instructed to do regardless if your gut feeling is telling you that it's not the right thing to do. Guilt can also be manifested in depression, stress, pressure, and anxiety.

Also let's not forget parenting guilt when you're pressured to make money and it takes away time from our children. Guilt makes us feel like horrible parents or it can even make us be semi mean to our children without even noticing. Guilt is a little bitch that must be smacked on the nose time after time. Give it time. It takes time. It's easy to make things worse when using too much force.

#Story199: Your money and my time faceoff.

Setting the appropriate price for this book has to do with my own beliefs and personal growth. It's such a beautiful thing being a self-publisher too. I can, without any filter, interact with my own truth and with those who find comfort in it. It's a beautiful thing that even an attempt to profit on those words turned out to somehow be a part of this journey and I feel so grateful to be guided through it all.

But is money worth the value of its content? This question was mostly for myself to answer. It's interesting to play with this answer as I'm fully aware that this book will impact every person that reads it. Nobody will walk away feeling the book didn't give them something. I've gone to some scary places to dig for some of the answers. I asked my followers how much I should price it. I let them and the Universe set the price, literally. "369 Stories" priced at $36.99. Now if you by any chance have accessed this book without paying for it, I need you to donate $36.99 to a charity or a cause of your own choice. I want you to continue your life journey by doing what is right. If you don't have the money at this time, do it when you can afford it. You don't need to inform me about it. This is for your own search and your own path.

"Greed & Lust - the old friends of human darkness sending its soldiers to throw weak punches. Every man in this world will have to face those demons sooner or later. If we don't, we better be ready to clean up our mess when the time comes to "report."

#Story200: Let's disconnect to connect.

On social media, we try to connect. In real life, we use similar technology to help us disconnect from each other. I don't think that we do it intentionally though. It's an energy block that we have to locate and dissolve. We still have a few things to figure out as far technology goes and how we make it serve us better, and to find a way to help us connect to each other in real life as well. We can't let anything create a distance between us and our children, friends, neighbors, co-workers...slowly but surely we'll get there.

#Story201: Love as your personal guide.

A wise person once said that life doesn't come with an instruction manual. My discoveries in life have showed me something different. Life comes with something better. It comes with a personal guide. It's the path of love and light. If we follow it, we'll always find our way out, around, or above all obstacles, issues, and darkness.

#Story202: Disappear to reappear.

To "disappear" doesn't always have to be dramatic or a big life-change. It's about making small adjustments that will allow you to redirect and shift inner energy that lead to personal growth. Growth is silent, but the results are extremely loud and powerful.

#Story203: I took a break from people's judgments.

I'm slowly unarchiving some of my past social media posts. At one point, I decided to archive them all during my journey to enlightenment. I wanted to simply break the energy pattern and allow myself to exist in a "gravity free zone" without any need to guard information, knowledge, or personal image. It was very liberating and truly contributed to my growth tremendously. I healed and I came back stronger.

#Story204: There is nothing to control and no need to understand everything.

Knowing that there is a higher power is so freeing in many ways. It's about silently knowing and understanding without any need to fully know or understand. Remember, we are not our mind. We are more than that. "The more than just our mind" is exactly the part that we don't always have to understand. It's more of a "gut feeling," an intuitive intelligence. It's there for us without our need to always be aware of it.

#Story205: Subjective truth.

I believe that we must walk through subjective realities (the direct manifestation of our free will) before we access the universal truth. The universal truth and harmony is a frequency, a certain vibration; and our ticket there is through personal growth, gaining wisdom, becoming more aware, becoming enlightened. Our actions in life determine how and when we get there, but there really is no rush. We all grow at a different pace. Let's not stress others or ourselves. We'll get there.

#Story206: Perspective without awareness.

It's not about perspective, but about awareness. How could someone trust their perspective if they have no awareness what that perspective means or where it comes from? Perspective is a constructed reality that mimics the universal blueprint, but without awareness.

#Story207: Happy Birthday To Me.

Turning 37 today. I wouldn't wanna change a thing about these past 36 years. I am celebrating my birthday by just being in the moment and not asking for or needing anything. No party, no cake, no presents. Just appreciating life that was given to me and appreciating birthday kisses and hugs from my family and all the birthday wishes from all of you. It's so beautiful to be able to just be. Why did it take me 37 years? How could I not see it?

#Story208: I don't have to know it all.

People who walk around, thinking and acting like they got it all figured out while never showing any vulnerability, are the most fragile individuals who lack the ability to face and address their own issues. They'll always try to defend their actions with blame, "facts," reasoning, and everything else that the ego keeps dear to itself. Sometimes, just acknowledging human vulnerability is a display of growth flexibility and personal strength. Without it, we can't go much further.

"It ran away from me. I feel that the fear fears me.
Not sure how that happened, but then again should I trust my feelings?"

#Story209: There is no You vs Your Mind. It's You + Your Mind.

Your mind doesn't put limits on you. You put limits on your mind. There is a reason. You are not supposed to grow faster than you're able to. It's your protection mechanism against yourself. Embrace it, but understand it.

#Story210: Create a problem, then offer a solution.

To motivational speakers and social media gurus: So you listen to people, you provide solutions, you motivate and inspire? What happens if it turns out that you're wrong about it all? Why take on so much responsibility when everyone is different? Also, why can't you tell people that they are great the way they are and no additional solutions are needed. Why make them feel like they are not enough? Why create problems and then offer solutions for them and stress people to follow your programs while you still search for your own answers? Just relax, take a break from it all, and give people a break from it all. They are fine the way they are.

#Story211: Sex, religion, and political discussions.

Discuss those topics to learn about yourself and how you react to people's reactions. Don't discuss those topics to prove people right/wrong.

For about a year, I've completely avoided engaging or supporting any political agendas. This is simply to purify my thoughts, emotions, and to get better clarity. Before, my political views were strongly influenced by my own fear. It was my fear of being judged, seen, and perceived in a certain way. I was trying to be "politically correct" just to protect my own image. Throughout my spiritual journey, everything has changed, including how I see politics, and politicians, but mostly how I see myself.

#Story212: My gift to me and to you.

This book is my gift to you as a thank you for helping me find some of the answers. But it's mainly a gift to myself and my family as I need a proper guide that makes sense to me and something to remind myself about as I go in life just in case I forget it. If I get off track, I want my wife to open the appropriate page and put it right in front of my face. Oh yes, I'll do it to her as well.

#Story213: Why? Says who?

Whenever you find yourself in an uncomfortable situation due to someone else verbally targeting you, just take a deep but silent breath, look them straight in the eye with a semi smirk and ask them: Why? Says who? They won't really have an answer and if they do, it will sound pushy and baseless. People who have answers won't make you feel uncomfortable UNLESS their intentions are to give you growth.

#Story214: The crappy story.

You need to go after yourself and your own bullshit as if it were the FBI, CIA, Interpol, and KGB all teamed up together to hunt your ass. Only an introspection like that will give you ability to recognize bullshit in others and see it for what it is.

I got tired of seeing my own crap in front of me. I knew that as long as I didn't clear it up, I wouldn't know whether what was in front of me was my own mistakes or other people's crap that was thrown at me.

#Story215: Healing through giving up.

The hardest part is not healing, but identifying what made you sick in the first place and giving up on it. If you are not ready to give up what is creating the greatest wound, then nobody can heal you. It's all about making that choice and using discipline to stick to the new path that you are on. Healing will take care of itself.

#Story216: Triggers make you suffer.

The cause to most of our suffering is ourselves. It's our ego. It's not other people, religion, politics, economic situation, money the system, or people who identify with those who trigger you. The people who trigger us to react, feel negative, and emotional, are messengers. They are messengers telling us that we have unhealed wounds to work on. If you get triggered, don't go after anyone or anything before you go after yourself first. Once you are healed, that's when you can approach a discussion and life in general from a neutral perspective and not from a triggered, emotional, and wounded place. Triggers make you suffer.

#Story217: Not tiny in the universe.

Those who believe that the Universe is in "outer space" may only discover "black holes" if they search for themselves in the outer world and space.

Once we become one with it, we are not tiny in this universe. We are only tiny if we are unaware about the greater purpose that we collectively are a part of. Those who live in denial about our universal purpose, are risking living this life believing that we are tiny and it's only the ego's accomplishments that make one appear big. Let's not fall for that mind-trick. Those who are somewhat aware, and who are on their journey of self-discovery, may quickly realize that the universe is within us and not on the outside. The outside world is the manifestation of our inner universe. Let's not lose our way in our search for ourselves in outer space.

#Story218: Hate & Fear.

Hate & Fear are your biggest enemies. They are very difficult to detect in yourself. The best way to discover those enemies is by observing how you feel towards certain individuals. If you have strong opinions and feelings about them, what they say and do, it has to do with your own issues. They are your mirror of your inner wellbeing. You don't go after those individuals. You go after yourself. Do you have to? No, you don't, but you will never know what is real and what is due to your projections. To put this in simple language: If you don't figure out this one, you are giving away all your power to other people. They control your life and you're playing the role of a puppet. It doesn't matter how rich, smart, or successful person is. A puppet is a puppet, playing in someone else's show...

#Story219: Consistency independence.

Your emotional and mental consistency should never depend on other people. It doesn't matter who those people are. Your best friend, parents, co-workers, people you look up to. You displaying an inconsistency based on dependence on how other people view this world should be a big concern for you.

#Story220: Force is a force.

I stumble upon emotionally damaged people on a daily basis who are seeking to destroy everything good in this world. The scariest thing is that they are not even aware of it. They walk around believing that they are doing good deeds as their actions are being controlled by agendas and forces who thrive on those damaged souls.

#Story221: Intentions can heal.

It's the healers' intentions that are powerful and healing. It's the tone in the words they speak that will carry a healing versus a damaging impact. This is in combination with the receiver's intellectual and spiritual openness to change.

#Story222: Attacking problems instead of distractions.

It's easy to get fooled to go after distractions instead of fighting the actual problems. If we don't locate the cause of the issue and cut it at its roots, we can spend all our energy fighting the symptoms but the problems will always reappear in a different shape. Instead of fighting food we should fight obesity, instead of fighting guns we fight mental illness, instead of fighting our spouse, we fight the issues that make us fight. Distractions always want us redirected. We need to know better.

#Story227: Experts vs ordinary people.

I spoke with a friend yesterday about podcasts. She mentioned a specific individual who runs a popular podcast and he brings famous "experts" to speak. Having a platform for other, already established "guards of programs and knowledge" to speak is something I consider brainwashing. If someone sees themselves as an individual with access to specific knowledge that can help other people, then there is no reason to fill the voids with other "experts." Bring "ordinary" people onboard. People who don't sell "knowledge" and "programs" turn out to be fountains of wisdom but only once they start trusting people and once they start opening up. I've now witnessed that for over a year with raw conversations with my followers. No "experts" are able to keep up with that. Experts simply guard what they know and they have limited ability to learn and see beyond that.

#Story228: With hate to love.

Everything in this world is about love. Even those who thrive on hate and use it as fuel to live and create, still seek love through hate. They are just not able to recognize it as their awareness is located in the higher context of self is blocked by rooted hate.

#Story229: Differing opinions.

Everyone has different opinions. But not everyone has the ability to rationalize or explain to others why their opinion is different from others. See my friend, that's what I consider to be different when it comes to different opinions. Seek people who can help further your opinions. Don't seek out people who will adopt your opinion.

> *"Seek people who can help*
> *further your opinions.*
> *Don't seek out people who*
> *will adopt your opinion."*

#Story230: Understanding others measures my growth.

My goal is to be able to understand everyone. By understanding others, I am able to understand myself. My goal is not to be able to be understood by everyone. That is not in my hands, it's in the hands of others and their own personal growth. We can only be responsible for ourselves. To be able to understand everyone means to be able to see through everyone and everything. That also includes being able to understand that some people are not able to understand beyond their strong opinions and beliefs that they guard. Two years ago, I used to get annoyed or sometimes frustrated if someone didn't agree with me. Now I smile and tell them that they are right. Everyone is right for what they know.

"Everyone is right
for what they know."

#Story231: Peace & Truth.

The truth is imprinted in every soul but not every person finds it.

It's our mind (Ego) that is in our way of finding peace and truth. The only way to bypass our mind is by being at peace with it. That can be accomplished by being at peace with everything else. There is no other way around it. The soul carries the truth, the ego carries the human flaws. We are in our own way most of the time. The more we grow, the more we heal, the less judgmental we are, the more filled with light and truth will we be.

#Story232: Staged lives shouldn't make you feel bad.

If you ever feel bad because others seem to be more popular or likeable, just remember that it's all staged. It's an act and not real life. I got a message in my inbox that reminded me to tell you about social media and what it truly means to be Insta and YouTube famous. It means nothing, even though it may seem like it means everything. It's all just a big illusion/show. With the right help, investment, and effort you too could have that fame. Now that you know that, go back to your life, and love every second of it because you are not missing out on anything. Trust me on this one.

#Story233: Pride.

There are two types of pride that need to be looked at. The first one is pride in yourself, meaning you having high opinion about yourself. I don't see any problems here, it's your right to think whatever you like about yourself and there are zero issues here. The second one is pride related to you and other people. Here, you seek validation and approval from others. If you sense that they don't align with your personal views and it evokes strong reactions and emotions in you, it can create certain problems. Even this pride is okay as well - you just need to recognize it and try to understand why it is important to you what other people think of you. Also, who are those people? Are there specific people that you care about or do you care about every single person in this world? I think once you start dissecting those things and lay them out, it will be easier for you to locate what is causing you problems.

#Story234: I salute you.

For many of you who were compelled to stick around and see the outcome, I truly salute you. I'm aware that what I posted posed a risk of offending many people, losing every follower, friend, heck even family members. But I know that somewhere deep inside, something was telling you to keep it cool, to wait and to see where it was headed. What you are now facing is not just my own growth but yours as well. I'm truly sorry if I ever hurt anyone. It was never my intention. And if you ever left without saying goodbye, whoever you are and wherever you are, I'd love to be friends again. I think I've grown.

#Story235: My views have no mission or agenda.

I can only help those who are already searching and who understand the concept of personal elevation and growth based on choices they make, facing and beating their own darkness, and mastering introspective analysis while using the outside world as a reference for their own growth. My views have no mission or agenda. They can only act as a mirror of self-reflection for your own growth. They can be a catalyst, but I can't allow my words to become an agenda. It would be against my own truth.

#Story236: Protecting children's minds.

We have to protect our children's minds and creativity by letting them learn what we know, but also making sure we tell them that's it's not the entire truth and that there is more that they will discover in life. Children are creative and imaginative, and discover knowledge faster if given the freedom to doubt and not just follow and obey the beliefs of others, including indoctrinated knowledge.

#Story237: Grounded & balanced.

Everything you discover in your spiritual journey must make rational sense to others, especially people that are close to you. Your discoveries must be useful for them and lead to a better quality of life for you and people around you. If not, than you may be off balance and too much in your own mind. You need to work on being grounded. Being grounded is a balance between your higher self and what keeps you grounded and balanced. In my case, it's my family and working out. We get our insights and wisdom from our higher self, but it still must be processed through the physical world (the physical realm) in order for that wisdom to be useful for us. It's a very simple, yet powerful, life philosophy.

#Story238: Labeling Is Not A Compliment.

Never try to label a person based on how you perceive them and then expect them to adopt and accept your label as a compliment. There are two main issues here: you not fully understanding the meaning of certain artificial virtues, and you not knowing the person you label with that virtue and how they perceive it.

#Story239: Taking it all away from me.

The truth is that I've been searching for a way to completely eliminate my ego or bring it down to an absolute minimum needed for existing in society as we know it. A part of that experiment was excluding my photos, videos, and my name from pretty much everything I posted over the last few months. It even came to a point where some people started asking if I still was alive. I just needed to go through that phase in order for me to know for sure what in this life is needed, what is optional, and what is necessary. Recently, I reached a point in my journey where I slowly started giving myself an identity again, simply because it was needed for existential balance. I've always been pretty extreme with everything, not always by choice. Sometimes it's the "Reverse Ego" that takes over. Yes it's another thing I've discovered over the last year or so. If you think that ego is bad, wait until you meet the Reverse Ego.

#Story240: Mind gymnastics.

Your brain is just like the rest of the body. It needs to exercise in order to stay vital and healthy. It's about not letting your mind fall into comfort zones. It's about not adopting knowledge, routines, programs, without questioning, analyzing, while always being open to receive more. The goal should not be to prove anything or to seek to discredit any evidence, facts or knowledge that already exists. The only goal should be to awaken certain parts of your mind that have genetically been asleep for many years.

#Story241: Comparing yourself.

Is it healthy to compare yourself to other people?

It serves a purpose, otherwise it wouldn't be relevant to compare yourself to others. Find out why you compare yourself to others. That's more important than finding out if it's healthy or not.

#Story242: Fatherly Fathers.

Having a father figure is a hit or a miss in every child's life. If the father understands the importance of his presence, actions, and how every word can impact his child throughout the rest of the child's life, then having a fatherly figure can help. For men, a fatherly figure is related to our identity, career choices, what we choose to become, the drive that comes from rooted passions such as becoming someone and something in life. We want something will impress our father figure only because they said something when we were children and we now want their love and recognition, without even being aware of it. This is very very dangerous, as we choose to live our life based on that one anchor (expectation and pressure) that we created in our head. Issues like this one are exactly why I believe it is important to start personal introspection and growth very early in life to try and catch all imbalances and anchors.

#Story243: War on religion.

I see so many people being mad, angry and frustrated at religion. As soon as I take a shallow dive into their emotional states towards religion, I quickly realize that their emotions come from negative experiences they had with people who were associated with those respective religions, and now those individuals are at war with them. I understand. It feels good. The truth is, religion will be ok without you, them, me, or anyone else.

Religion was created to help people. It's the original simulation of the truth. Meaning, religion carries a lot of hidden human and existential truth in it. Why let those people who mistreated you turn your entire life into a war against teachings that were originally created for the right reasons? You don't have to follow any structure or let anyone else dictate how you connect to God or what parts of religion you use for your personal growth and reference. You free yourself from religion and then you use what serves you. Remember that anything you fight in life, you will eventually become, but for all the wrong reasons.

#Story244: Question: Why do I cheat on my boyfriend?

Answer: You have rooted, unhealed wounds that you're not aware of. You keep searching for something or someone but you don't know what or who. You are simply trying to fill a void. Remember that you're hurting yourself the most when searching for life answers through sex.

#Story245: Your child.

1. Listen to your child.
2. Hear your child.
3. See your child.
4. Heal your child.
5. Know your child.
6. Trust your child.
7. Be one with your child.
8. Apologize when you're wrong and admit that you've made a mistake.
9. Do not assume that you are smarter solely because you are older.
10. Be affectionate as much as possible. This releases hormones and will make your child stronger, smarter, and more immune to many diseases.
11. Remember that the baby industry is an industry and they will do everything they can to make you feel like an awful parent and that you need the crap they try to sell to you, including information. Don't fall for it. Most of it is optional. Your child needs your love, food, and shelter.

"It's the self-inflicted worry, stress, pressure, and guilt about providing what we believe is necessary
for our children's future while forgetting to give our children the real superpower, awareness."

#Story246: Good, bad, right, wrong.

It helps sometimes to live in dualism, governed by rights and wrongs, but we have reached a level of pressure where right and wrong no longer work as seamlessly as they used to. We have reached a point in our civilization where we need to understand and we need to be understood. By understanding causes to issues and by knowing that we can fix things in life and that God still loves us is honestly all we need to be able to find our truth (our way) in life. All we need is someone to reassure us that we are not a total failure and that it's not our fault for everything bad that is happening in our own lives and around us. Not everything is black or white. The truth is in the grays.

#Story247: What does slowing down in life mean?

It means a realization that most of the things that I once found to be important in life suddenly became less relevant. God presents you a new path in life that requires certain life adjustments and a dive into the unknown. Each new battle you win against the darkness gives you wings to fly into new elevated dimensions in life.

Slowing down in life doesn't always means stagnation but rather a fast-track to a more fulfilled, successful, and happier life. It's a lost wisdom and a way of living that is hidden from those who choose or get tricked to fall for certain temptations in life.

#Story248: We are only responsible for ourselves.

(This is a reply to a follower who tried to push me to take the responsibility of awakening the masses. The following story is related to me pushing away guilt and pressure to do so.)

All my decisions in life nowadays are based on my personal peace, balance, and approach to morals and ethics that I've set for myself. It has nothing to do with other people. My family, God, and myself are my entire world. Other things are becoming secondary and optional. It's a simple life-philosophy that I've discovered during this journey. Anything else would be an act of ego and distortion of my truth.

It's liberating being able to stop trying to please others. I try to please myself instead. Also a realization that I don't owe anything to anyone else but to myself and my own family. My evaluations and approach to what I consider to be morally correct and business lucrative ideas have nothing to do with other people, but with my own beliefs. Also, broader awareness or awakening is not a trend, nor is it my responsibility. Whatever is a part of God's plan will happen and people's egos don't have to always interfere and take on a bigger responsibility.

#Story249: Ego seeks knowledge. Soul seeks answers.

Enlightenment is not about power. It's about finding love, peace, and harmony in life. Ego seeks knowledge. Soul seeks answers. They both need to be balanced and in harmony. Nobody can give you enlightenment. It's your personal choices you make in life that can either bring you closer to your higher self or take you further away from your truth. Also, your ability to be vulnerable plays a big part. If we constantly keep our guard up, we can never make room for light and love to come in. Vulnerability in your search for answers, and your ability to monitor your inner peace can all help you on your path to enlightenment.

"We don't need to know people's motives. It's not about knowing. Wisdom is about being able to see through things and people. Motives change faster than people."

#Story250: Pressure to depression.

It turns out that one of the greatest causes of depression is the pressure that people put on others. They are mostly career oriented. It's mainly programs that ask you: "So what do you do?" "How much do you make" "Hey so what's new with your job"...Let it go, leave people alone. People don't have to do anything else, but exist.

"Ego seeks knowledge.
Soul seeks answers."

#Story251: Spill yourself out.

How do you spill yourself out more and let more light in? By trying to not be judgmental - and by that I don't mean to hide away from judging but rather, by facing it and trying to understand that it's not the whole truth. Each time we judge something or someone we set a limit for how much light is able to get in.

#Story252: Old way vs new way.

How can you know the difference between the old way and the new way? There is no need to confuse yourself and create another block. Just be human and live your life without holding back. If you react in a way that you or others find disruptive, take a step back and analyze. Keep it simple and real. Always stay true to yourself if you want to reach the truth. You can't reach the truth through someone else's truth.

#Story253: Why seek my approval?

So many of you asked for my opinion about
books, quotes, solutions, gurus...If it appeals to
you, why do you need someone else's opinion?
It will only confuse you. If something relates to
you, there is no need to seek further until those
things no longer relate to you.

"As long as we keep seeking for answers solely
on the surface in the physical world we will
never know what is 'real and important'
and what is just a trick (illusion)."

#Story254: Only love overwrites certitude and fear.

If certitude and fear aren't real (and in my world they are not real), is control even possible? Could it be something else? A trick perhaps? Designed by the negative force (The Devil aka the Ego)?

AHA! Some are controlled (programmed) without even recognizing it and we will have no ability to pull them out of that dimension. There is only one way out (up) to higher context of self and that is LOVE. Basically it's the only power that can overwrite everything else that was created by the darkness and that enslaves our human minds. Why Love? Because the Love dimension is the closest we can get to God while on Earth!

#Story255: Creating new energy patterns.

We can't only feed into what we already know and what we are used to. In order to grow and learn new things, we must sometimes introduce new experiences, new perspectives, new thoughts, and opinions. Only then can things open up for us. Comfort zones will eventually lead to discomfort. Get comfortable being uncomfortable on your own terms instead.

#Story256: Saving myself from myself.

God created us out of love, meaning God does everything he can to seamlessly save his children from their own choices. When I look back at my life, it's easy to see that God has been fighting for me and been by my side all these years. It's only now, at the age of 37 that I'm able to see it. I can see that all decisions I have made in my life that came out of love and that followed the path of love, are the decisions that helped me transcend into the higher context of self and free myself from the heavy chains of everything that wasn't me.

#Story257: I want to trust science.

I'd like to see the science community start to put people, people's beliefs, and their voice before titles, facts, ego, and statistics. Science is important, but it's time to take a step back and take a philosophical approach for a little way. We can't let scientists turn us into programmed individuals with limited ability to think freely and outside of statistics, hypotheses, and research papers. Certain things in life can't be justified or explained with facts that may be as equally distorted as their own limitations when it comes to thinking outside of what is already known.

Many students are burned out, forced to learn blind facts without having a broader understanding of themselves and what purpose their knowledge will one day serve. I want to trust science, but I hope it will take a more human and philosophical approach so it doesn't forget what purpose it serves.

"Nobody should feel that they don't have the right to be right."

#Story258: There is no rainbow or is there?

You see a rainbow. It's colorful and it's arched. It doesn't even exist as we are only able to perceive it as nerve signals sent to our brain from our retinas through chemical reactions stimulated by different wavelengths of light reflected and refracted through water (so we think). We'll never reach a rainbow's end. But we see it, so it's real? Does it even matter? Regardless if one chooses to believe in rainbows or not, the person should be allowed to believe so and nobody should be judged for their beliefs. It's about our freedom to think and not just accept program after program. As for now, we have no visual ability to perceive the shape of earth and those who choose to believe that the earth is round or flat can both be right. Many people care about being right but fail to understand that facts are not equal to the truth. Just like justice is not equal with the truth. Justice and Facts are constructed simulations of the truth, but they are not always true. Also, in order to be right, one must make rational sense that is broadly accepted, understood, useful and not taking away anything from anyone, including our freedom to speak, and express ourselves.

"Acknowledging someone else's knowledge doesn't take your knowledge away from you."

#Story259: Hate and pain are "You-Niversal."

Yes, hate and pain are universal. It's just "packaged" and presented in different ways. The only way to stop or reverse it, is to be able to recognize it, identify its origins, and know how to not feed into it. What triggers you, triggers others as well. Because you have the same triggers, doesn't mean that the healing journey is the same. Your journey is your own even though the pain and hate are universal.

"Let's try to understand that good intentions can still be harmful if they come from a blind place."

#Story260: The Return.

Let's play with the idea that we have the ability to return to the original version of humans, as God created us in the Garden of Eden. It's obviously a mental journey of personal growth. I believe it's doable in one's lifetime for those who find it in their hearts. A person is only responsible for his or her own actions and the person doesn't have to worry about the rest of the world and how the world changes. We change the world by changing our own world.

"Our existence is more than what our five senses perceive. For example you are able to perceive a rainbow but you'll never reach a rainbow's end."

#Story261: Losing weight.

Most of the time it's not our body weight we need to lose. It's the weight of pressure, guilt, shame, fear, social norms, indoctrination, hate, anger, expectations, and worry.

#Story262: Self-Help Books.

Why are they called Self-Help books if they come with instruction manuals written by other people *telling you* how to help yourself? Self-help is *you helping yourself* without other people's influence other than material provided for self-reflection. Watch out for recycled energy that doesn't bypass your own spiritual and intellectual levels that you already have access to. Consider trusting yourself more when it comes to knowing yourself than letting others tell you about knowing yourself.

#Story263: Heads up for impurity.

Always be on the lookout for the following words in spiritual messages or any messages in general:
Control
Command
Must
Stop
Punishment
Those are threats that you will be punished or that you will miss out on something if you don't do this or that (I.e. pray, buy something, attend something). Direct commands and threats are driven by agendas and personal projections.

"It's not important what people ask from you.
What matters is recognizing your own
strength and weakness when answering."

#Story264: Indecisiveness.

Your indecisiveness comes from somewhere deeper. I suggest you look at your childhood and people who were important in your life. Did they let you make your own choices or did they create a block in you by not letting you make any of your choices, even the simplest ones? If you can locate this, it will help you make your choices in life much easier.

#Story265: Generosity.

Generosity is an instant product of love and absence of greed. It shouldn't be determined by any scale but rather, by a person's heart. A person should genuinely find it in themselves to give, rather than being directed or forced to give money either through obligation or guilt. There already exists a social structure and taxes through what we all contribute for mutually agreed social welfare and infrastructure. Monetary contributions have nothing to do with the truth. Generosity, on the other hand, does.

#Story266: Fighting for a cause.

If you choose to fight for a cause and become an activist, make sure to be completely healed first. If you go in the battle wounded, you will be leaving traces of havoc wherever you go. If you fight against what hurt you without being fully healed, you aren't free from it, you're just on the opposite side of the equation still belonging to the same darkness.

#Story267: Loyalty.

Loyalty is a product of trust between two people. Loyalty is not a personal quality. It should not be confused with obedience. Loyalty can't be constructed, meaning you're equally responsible for it as the other person is. It's not a one-way street.

#Story268: Doubt wins when ego speaks.

1. An individual makes some personal growth and starts discovering things he never experienced before. He gets excited and starts sharing it with the rest of the world.

2. Instead of continuing to grow, he sees potential to make a name for himself by lying to himself that he wants to help people by presenting his discoveries.

3. The spirit begs him saying "No, wait."

4. He can't wait. As he starts putting himself out there completely vulnerable, he gets attacked from every side without strength to defend himself or his discoveries.

5. The spirit "hides."

6. Doubt wins and the person goes back to what the ego perceives as normal in society.

#Story269: Motivation needs no motivation.

Truth doesn't need decoration and marketing. It's the energy shifts within us (growth) that are the biggest motivators. Motivation should be internal and not come from external people presented as idols, speakers, or pastors...Many are preaching distorted wisdom while still searching for their own answers.

"Sometimes we just need to let go of that need to know how long or how far we have to go. That's when major shifts start to magically happen."

#Story270: Question: Is making profit bad?

Answer: It's not really about personal gain or profit, but about greed. The tricky part is to fully embrace the truth as one chooses to exist and live in the physical world *within* the system built on greed. It's about finding a balanced solution between earning a living, growing in all aspects of life, helping others grow, and find their light. If one's choices create opportunities that lead to profit, I see nothing wrong with it.

#Story271: Practicing Sex should not be an obligation.

Who says that you must have sex with your partner? It's just another social norm that is broadly accepted and yet nobody can explain why. Love should not be dependent on sexual practices, but rather be an optional choice as a natural expression of physical and spiritual attraction between two individuals.

Many speak about protecting personal energies and peace, but nobody speaks about protecting one's sexual energy. Let me remind you that sexual energy is a powerful life force that can create life. Also, let me remind you, that such a force can also destroy a life.

#Story272: Dreams are never just dreams.

Dreams are communication interferences between our spiritual and physical world that appear as involuntary images, sensations, emotions, and thought glitches during sleep. They are created due to energy clogging (imbalances) in energy vortexes in our body where electrical vibrations pass through on their way to the pineal gland where the energy exchange/communication between the two worlds occur. The energy blocks that create glitches are accumulated through our experiences in the physical world when we are awake. The glitches can either be pleasant (dreams) or distressing (nightmares).

I don't see any reason or need to remember any of our dreams. I find no importance in them other than seeing it as a signal that we may need to adjust certain things in life if nightmares are repetitive. It's mostly stress and anxiety that cause them.

#Story273: Doing "the right thing" is not a feeling.

I've talked about this one before and there is only one way to be able to measure the strength of our relationship with God. It's not related to other people, their set of rules, fears or teachings. It simply has to do with our own balance. Nothing else.

Experiencing life should not be done in fear for God's punishment. Morals were artificially created by humanity, partially for order and control. They may have originally been created with good intentions, but they have been distorted since then and it has taken us far, far away from the truth and from God. Those who find God no longer rely on social norms, rules, or morals. They are simply guided by light and they choose to live their life that brings them closer to their peace and personal balance. Doing "the right thing" simply becomes an energy pattern and not a programmed act of our ego.

#Story274: Your friends are not you.

Your friends' understanding of things is their own. Yours is yours. Regardless of how well you may think that you know people around you, remember that you don't know their journey and what God has planned for them. Always trust your own intuition. Don't let your mind trick you. Our ego is easily manipulated by the Devil. Our intuition is not.

People in our life should matter to us, but what they think and what they know should matter less, specifically if they try to push their views and perspectives.

"Sometimes we don't need to know answers. We just need to be aware of shifts of change."

#Story275: Parent & spouse are not roles to me.

It just is, it's a part of me just like breathing. I didn't come to the choice of having children. It was a natural product of love between my wife and I, expressed through passionate and intimate physical, spiritual, and sexual fusion one night. I don't remember making any choices. I just remember that it was special. It's called life. We try to label phases of our life and its experiences. I prefer to just live and love! Everything else falls into its place.

#Story276: Question: What is your opinion on Sexy IG girls that tempt men from a guy's perspective?

Answer: My perspective is not a guy's perspective. It's simply a neutral objective perspective. If I were giving you a "guy's perspective" it would be a projection. There is a constant struggle between light and dark in every man's life. It does none of us any good to focus on one side without acknowledging the presence of the other. The reason why men fall for the lustful presentation of other women (I.e. sexy IG girls) is because they are still trapped in rooted lower vibration energies that carry hidden memories from childhood, in most cases related to a female figure.

As adults, there is a clear behavioral pattern and search for ways to fill the emptiness that is a product of personal darkness that we never take the time to face. Our ability to see beyond the sexual presentation is blurred and suppressed. Women, on the other hand, thrive on this weakness as they get attention and validation and they enjoy it UNTIL they too fall "victim" for the same pain that they unknowingly caused others.

"Nobody should be blamed for emotional pain that has unknown roots."

#Story277: Tired of being too serious.

I keep catching myself for being too serious or too much in my head nowadays. It's not necessary and honestly not healthy. Nothing is as refreshing as taking a sharp turn from wise and smart to childish and playful.

#Story278: Just playing a role.

People who play different roles in everyday life always run out of lines sooner or later. When that day comes, instead of making a U-turn to start to search for answers within, they turn themselves to offered solutions and programs that are presented to them as the path to ultimate happiness and success. It's nothing else but just another role with additional lines they are being assigned to play. This continues until they get replaced with other more suitable actors of life.

#Story279: Surface is a trap.

There is no race, color, or religion. We all come from the same, belong to the same, and we will return to the same source. Those separations were created by us for various reasons. When you get your passport, your race, color, and height are listed but it doesn't say where in life we are mentally, spiritually, or emotionally because it's individual and personal.

So if you see yourself as an individual, then why do you see color and race? The less surface you see in others and the more truth and soul you start seeing in people, the closer you are to your truth. Don't get distracted by yourself. It's just another trap, another test stopping you from growth and from accessing the well-hidden and tucked away truth about everything you need to know.

#Story280: Pursuit of truth.

Don't expect the truth to be taught to the masses. Oh no, my friend. It's a journey of solitude. You may walk together with the masses, but don't get distracted by leaning on anyone or anything as there is no real support there. Pursuit of the truth is the most personal thing you've experienced. Every second of your life, every thought you think, every decision you make, big or small. The surface remains the same as you walk with the masses, but inside yourself there is a whole universe that only you have a ticket to.

#Story281: Be cautious and pay attention.

Pay attention to people around you. Not because you should change anyone but because they can serve as a mirror of self-reflection. If you're completely comfortable around people who have fully accepted and embraced a work-eat-sleep-survive, life cycle without ever asking what they are doing here on earth, who they truly are, or have zero interest in the deeper meaning of life; see it as a red flag as you have fallen into the biggest trap of this life. You need to automatically have an "out of self" extreme intro and extrospection of your entire life. No panic or instant changes needed. Start by asking some deeper questions. This will open up some gateways for further steps that you need to take from there.

#Story282: Who are you?

If you can answer who you are without mentioning your name, job, career, nationality, religion, or friends, you're on the right path.

"A poet is someone who knows how to extract brightness from darkness through the art of writing."

#Story283: My daughter is lucky, but I'm luckier.

It would be so much harder for me to find my peace and balance without fully embracing my role as a parent. Being there for my daughter the way she needs me and not the way I believe that she needs me. Finding a way to enter her world and being a part of it when with her, while guiding her towards mine, is the most precious and valuable personal growth experience for me.

#Story284: Using programs to deprogram.

The risk is falling into traps of deprogramming patterns and adopting it as a lifestyle.

The best option is to live and experience life, and also, through encounters with people and situations while doing a proper introspective analytical evaluation of your own behavior, reactions, and emotional states. Keeping things as organic as possible is the healthiest way to grow.

#Story285: Kids need their parents more than their money.

Children are growing up deprived from love while their parents are tricked into believing that they need to be away from their children, working and making money, in order to give them happiness and a better life. The truth is, we all got screwed in a way. Some kids turn out fine as they enter their adulthood, but most have to spend a bigger portion of their lives trying to locate what needs to be fixed emotionally and mentally while seeking love in strangers, careers, politics, sports teams , boyfriends, girlfriends, employers, authorities, and last but not least, social media validation.

#Story286: We are never alone.

We are never alone when we are alone. We can only be alone when we are around people who don't walk the same path as we do. It's important to remember that we should not try to change people. We should only try to change our own circumstances that are more aligned with our journey and where we are in life. The reason why we often feel better alone than surrounded by other people is because we are never really alone. Everything around us is alive and carries vibrations and valuable information. The universe and God try to speak to us, but we rarely tune in as it's always loud around us and in our heads. And when we listen, we try to overthink everything by trying too hard to understand it all. Sometimes we just need to let it all go and just be. The answers will come later. We just need to be open to accept that there is more than what it appears to our senses. We just need to tune in and be ready to receive.

#Story287: A man of no style.

Someone commented today that they liked my new style. The truth is, I no longer have a style. I completely let my surface presentation be steered by my inner transformation. Inner energy shifts transform one's entire outer world as well. It's so powerful and real that only a little over a year ago, I would not even know what all of this even meant.

#Story288: Don't take it personal.

Never get flattered, upset, personal, or emotional when communicating with me. Connecting to many of you is my way of raw communication with people from all walks of life about various topics. It's just my little way of doing field research for various topics, books, and teachings. Remember that I only speak to what you give me and not you as a person. Most of the time I don't know your names or how you look like and it doesn't even matter to me. I just hope we can both grow from each interaction.

#Story289: Calm your anger. Tame your projection.

(A part of a conversation with a female follower seeking advice about men who she feels let her down by cheating.)

It sounds like you were cheated on or you have difficulty finding love because you don't look for love, you look for men who can feed into your emotional and sexual state without your awareness. Because of this, you don't trust men. Perhaps you don't realize that you don't have to do all those things you listed in order for you to find love. Perhaps if you can let go of your anger and fighting this battle that doesn't exist, you will be able to find more peace in everything.

It's the career that forces women to choose between serving the wheel instead of serving their own life while living in peace with themselves and in love. This shift happened during/after the Industrial Revolution.

You will need to make some energy shifts within yourself in order for you to recognize a different type of energy (in men) than what you currently attract. You're only able to recognize men and love through sexual attraction and emotional needs hidden in your root issues.

You have created this war in your head but that war doesn't even exist. It only exists in your head. And because there are other women who have similar issues, you group yourself with them through social media and even different type of female activism so it appears like you're not alone and that your issues are very common. You're in fact only hurting yourself and your own life with this "battle."

> *"Nothing can hurt you as much*
> *as your own expectations."*

#Story290: Planting seeds.

Planting a seed and growing isn't at first, visible or impressive to those who can't see beyond the surface. Once you start penetrating deep and spreading your roots quietly, boom, the next thing you know you've grown into a beautiful, nutritious, and healthy enlightened God's creation.

#Story291: Rewarding your ego to keep your soul enslaved.

They'll try to reward your ego to keep your creativity enslaved by putting pressure on you with expectations that comes with the reward. Resisting temptation is hard as it comes in different shapes, but it's truly freeing to be able to say no sometimes.

#Story292: Peer Pressure.

It's not about blocking peer pressure but rather about recognizing it, being able to neutrally rationalize and think about so we don't have to bend for it, but the other way around. It's all about having that ability and awareness to categorize the type of energy that is coming at us, its intentions and how it's affecting us, our personal peace and growth.

> *"You can try to show some people how to walk on water and they'll ask you to show them how to drown instead."*

#Story293: We are not strangers, we are just pretending.

What does being a stranger mean anyway? Being close to people is more than just knowing them for a long time. If we all dared to be ourselves constantly, we would realize that we would never have to be alone in this world. It's our guard and masks/facades that are stopping us from connecting to people that we should be connecting to.

So many of you share the same issues. Sometimes I click on your profiles and I realize that the presentation is different from what you all are going through. Sometimes I wonder how the world would look like if we all dared to bring our depth to the surface. Something is telling me that our fear is stopping us from connecting, healing, and living.

#Story294: Do not walk away.

Don't walk away from problems, bad vibes, people who try to do you harm. Your issues will not disappear. You will meet the same type of energy in different bodies wherever you go, unless you hold your ground and stand up for yourself. If you believe that you have been treated wrong, you have nothing to worry about. Everything bends for the truth. You just need to embrace it and become it. The rest will be taken care of one way or another. Hold your ground, stand up for yourself, and for what's right or keep "walking away" the rest of your life. Let bad vibes and people walk away from your truth. Trust me, nothing can be as powerful as the Wrath of Truth coming after those who fear it. Don't let your mind play tricks on you with a fear that doesn't even exist. The real fear is with those who try to harm you...Go after it!

#Story295: Are you truly lucky?

Luck is a subjective thing. What you consider to be lucky, someone else may find to be misfortune. The beauty of life is that you get to set your own paradigms and define everything that is important to you in your lifetime. Why let someone else set a reference point for your personal journey?

#Story296: My stories, but your life and choices.

There is no agenda, personal projections, or need from my side for you to accept or change anything in your life by reading this book. You're fully in charge of all your choices. I'm just looking to point the spotlight at things that you normally wouldn't look at for various reasons. Things I bring up are random. They get put in front of me for different reasons and I present what I know and how I see it. If I ever projected or mixed personal emotions, I would consider it a failure from my side and regression in my personal growth and journey.

#Story297: Birth-Control Pills.

Let's just stay at the literal meaning of those three world: BIRTH. CONTROL. PILLS.

It's simple my friends. Each time we try to control nature, it backfires badly.

Anything that needs control is bad news and always has been. Imagine giving so much power to a pill that it can actually control, modify, and even eliminate the outcome of your future. How do you really know that those evil things don't impact your genetic code that may be affecting your children, grandchildren and beyond. Let's be careful.

Do your research, there is enough information out there. You need to know that you absolutely don't need to take those pills, no matter what some doctor tells you or prescribes. They are just people too, most of them equally or more asleep than the general public. You are completely in charge of your own body and life. Don't make it easy for any pharmaceutical company! Question. Research. Speak up. Share Your Story.

#Story298: Natural Healing.

I think when it comes to any conditions, our bodies have the ability to naturally heal itself. I believe that when our internal physical self becomes misaligned with our true self, it becomes manifested in various ailments. So many physical conditions are just manifestations of our inner well-being. Many medications are just Band-Aids for hemorrhage and the problem is they don't really fix the source of the problem, and they also have side effects. Healing and health will only happen when it happens from within. The current problem with medical education is that it focuses on collecting symptoms, then trying to label them with a diagnosis and then assign a medication. But the system doesn't teach how dig deeper to the root of an issue. Most health care providers can't do this for themselves, so how are they able to help others do this too? So the health care system operates on the surface with equations, statistics, and pills. We shouldn't undermine the importance of medication and pharmaceutical research, but we also shouldn't undermine the importance of natural healing and putting more effort and resources in discovering more, not going further away from it.

#Story299: How you see me is not how I see myself.

I just want to be me for a while without labeling or categorizing. I just want to be without being anything or anyone. During this journey you've tried to call me everything from a philosopher, inspirational speaker, guru, an angel, a bullshitter... But honestly for now I just want to be and I'll take it from here when the dust settles.

#Story300: Question: Is having children a must to feel accomplished?

(A question from a female follower.)

Feeling unaccomplished has to do with your mind and thoughts that are related to social conditioning by the definitions of what a woman should be like. Your existence, just the way you are, is an accomplishment itself. Your purpose in life is not related to social conditioning, but to God's plan. That is your real and true purpose. You will be guided as you go, just listen to your intuition and don't always worry about what your mind tells you. We are all here for a specific reason and I can't see why reproduction would be a part of everyone's purpose.

#Story301: Question: Why do you come across as so arrogant?

How can you be so sure that you don't see your own flaws in me? Figure that one out before you judge.

From Merriam-Webster Website: *Arrogance: "an attitude of superiority manifested in an overbearing manner or in presumptuous claims or assumptions."*

I took 48 seconds (I timed it) to corner myself and properly reflect on my behavior that may have come across as arrogant. It's a big hobby of mine to observe myself. It looks like you may be looking at your own shadow when pointing your words at me. I suggest you take some time and write a personal letter to your ego telling it to reconsider attributing its qualities to others while fighting for its own agenda.

#Story302: What is your biggest insecurity?

   For a big part of my life I was very insecure. From a young age, I created goals, put pressure and expectations on myself to become a man and achieve things that I believed would give me validation from people I looked up to at the time. I could never find fulfillment no matter how much attention I got, how much money I made, or how good I looked. Luckily, at one point I said enough is enough. I decided to look deep into myself and see what was missing, who I truly was, and what I truly wanted without social attachment, pushed away identities that were leading to imbalance and losing connection to myself. Friendships, relationships, businesses, insecurities, anger, grudges, and expectations: these were all toxic in my world.

#Story303: A note to my enemies.

I never knew that my biggest enemies were invisible. Until I faced all of them, I couldn't see clearly who my enemies are. How could I be so blind? To my invisible enemies; greed, lust, anger, pride, hate, resentment, expectations, worry, anxiety, slander, fear, egoism, I know you're reading and I want to let you know that I'm watching you. It's safest for you keep your distance.

#Story304: My strongest weapon.

Sometimes I wonder if my strongest weapon is my refusal to ever see myself as broken and helpless but rather as growing and healing. I don't want to ever become comfortable being a victim of my own life.

#Story305: Social Media.

It is such a beautiful way to channel our disobedient rebellious nature through social media. For the first time in human history (as far as there are any records) we have found a way around it all; parents, school, religion, government, the system...and we have given ourselves a voice with a platform, waiting for us to be heard. It's beautiful, it's wonderful, it feels great, it feels wonderful. But let's not forget that even here we need to find our balance as social media is a strong energy pull. If we are not cautious, the next thing you know we are sinking in our own quicksand without anything to hold on to. Internet and social media is still new and for many it doesn't feel like "real life" but it is as real as anything else. Energy is energy. Social Media doesn't need a break from you, but you need a break from it. Make sure to detox yourself from it for at least four weeks. As I'm writing this, I just announced on my Instagram page that I'm taking a break from social media and the internet in general June 1st - July 1st. I already feel that I'm freed from its strong pull, but something tells me that there are a few things to catch in myself that are hanging over my mind and I want to see what I discover. I want to see if there are any dangers in constantly feeding into my follower's needs and wants and feeding into my own needs and wants. Let me see what I can catch. Like anything else in life, we need to set rules and boundaries for ourselves with social media. It's easy to get sucked into various energy patterns without even noticing.

#Story306: Betrayal.

It turns out that your silent expectations collided with my own silent plans. Who is to blame? Do I owe you to tell you personal plans that don't involve you? But I'd certainly not mind if you are vocal about your expectations that involve me. See my friend, betrayal is your own demons messing with your mind, I don't really want it over here, I'm good.

#Story307: How did you find your calling?

I never stopped seeking and it finally found me. It was that silent knowing without knowing. That feeling of being unsettled, unfulfilled, even when I should have felt completely fulfilled. I knew that there was more, but I didn't know what that was. I'm happy I followed my gut and my heart those times when my mind couldn't help me figure things out. I knew that there was a higher order and I didn't let my mind create disorder. Slowly. but surely, my calling was revealed to me. But I also feel like that my life could have been good either way, I could have chosen to stay where I was so many times and it could have been great. Honestly, I just think that I'm over-ambitious sometimes.

#Story308: What's the key to succeed in business?

To believe in your business as much as you believe in yourself and to know its possibilities and limitations as much as you know yours. Be very clear and honest with yourself. Your business will always be a manifestation of your personal inner world. Also make sure that your motivation comes from the right place of purity and the right intentions rather than greed and desire for power, if we fall for those two tricks, it will give us a ton of headache sooner or later.

#Story309: Have you ever felt left out of society?

Never. Society doesn't owe me a thing and never has. We are all a part of it and have a chance to exit it anytime. We choose to stay because there is no better alternative. We need to find ways how to utilize society and the system, but also to contribute and give back to it. There is nobody to blame for anything and nobody to point fingers at.

#Story310: Question from a follower: Do you have any advice on my judgement day anxiety?

Every day is a judgment day...we judge and we are being judged. The anxiety comes from our fear of the unknown. We need to trust the higher power (God) and that there is an order above it all. Things that we don't need to control and things that we can't comprehend. Certain things just are. Here and now is all that we have to focus on. It's a mind trick to let other thoughts pull you away. Try to stay grounded. Don't let your thoughts pull you away. That's anxiety that is protecting you from going too far away from this life that we are supposed to live. Anxiety is forcing you to look for ways to stay balanced right here where you are. Judgment day shouldn't be seen as a physical matter. It's a spiritual battle. Let God fight it for us. We can only be in charge of our own life, thoughts and actions. Judgment day could have already passed without us even knowing. God is seamless, just like his mercy is.

Like every other spiritual teaching, we need to interpret spiritual and religious metaphors in our own way that leads to peace and harmony and not to inner war and disruption within us. We just have to find peace, love and fulfillment; that's what it's all about.

#Story311: Anxiety.

Anxiety should be acknowledged and embraced as our protector. It's telling us that our mind is pulling us away from the truth and reality with its own conspiracy theories about our future. We just really have to embrace the here and now and try to stay grounded. It's the balance between the higher and lower self that is the key.

#Story312: Do you regret anything?

Not necessarily. Maybe I wish I didn't hurt some people in my life unintentionally. Sometimes I analyze and question some choices I've made in my life, but I always come to the same answer. The choices were a product of my desire to search for my own path and answers that nobody else could give me but myself. I never intentionally wanted to harm myself or anyone else with any of my choices, but now I do realize that sometimes we hurt people around us when we blindly focus on things in life that don't even matter.

#Story313: Hi Friend.

Most of you I'll never meet in person, and yet here I am hoping to make an impact on your life and I can feel it's importance. When your intentions are pure, you never have to worry if your actions will help anyone. You never know how big of an impact a small thing can have on others.

#Story314: Be my Valentine.

This is the day people exchange pre-phrased and pre-quoted cards, and give candy and flowers to each other. It would be more profound if people actually were praising love and not being victims of pressure, expectation, or self-inflicted Valentine's Day love depression that comes from loneliness, not feeling loved enough, and other factors. Let's try to find out the real truth behind the Valentine's Day celebration that has partially defined "the concept of modern love." There are two historical events that have given birth to this holiday and they both date back to the ancient Romans.

One story says that Valentine was a priest who served during third century Rome. Emperor Claudius II felt that soldiers who were single were better than those with families. He then he outlawed marriage for young men. Valentine felt that this was unjust and continued to marry soldiers. When Valentine's actions were discovered, Claudius ordered his execution on February 14.

Another celebration is traced back to Lupercalia. It was a pre-Roman annual festival that was believed to promote health and fertility and was celebrated between February 13 and 15th. Don't you find it incredible how religious programs even to this day, affect our intimacy and love life? Even though it's very commercialized today, the spirit of its celebration and intention is still the same: To control people's free will and emotional well-being.

> *"Winning over your lower self is*
> *a sacred deity-like power.*
> *With your mind free of fear*
> *and lustful desires, you gain*
> *flawless freedom and endless*
> *strength to devote to your*
> *life's missions."*

#Story315: About to start a family. I'm really nervous about life changes. How do you adjust?

As you go through the motions of life, your fear, that is now showing up as nervousness, will slowly be releasing you. Fear always finds its ways to hold us back and distracts us from doing what's best for us.

#Story316: Do you participate in any charity work?

Charity is not a participation. Charity is one's ability to recognize important issues and compassionately contribute to solving those issues. What you are talking about is contributing through accepting what someone else tells you is *needed* for the rest of the world. My life has completely become about giving, but it's giving on my own terms.

#Story317: Help ourselves or help others?

Once you've truly found a way to help yourself, others will find you.

#Story318: How can you cope with loneliness? How can you talk about your demons?

By talking with someone you trust (or decided to trust) and letting all your "demons" resurface. If you don't have anyone to talk to, write everything down and read it out loud while standing in front of a mirror. From there you'll be guided by your good spirit that is always fighting for you. Just meet him halfway.

#Story319: What advice you would tell your younger self?

You're exactly where you are supposed to be, headed to where you are meant to be. There is no other way.

#Story320: What does "freedom" mean to you?

To have full existential awareness with a clear definition of my role in the society, based on personal drive and motivation that are completely internal, as a product of a balanced mental, physical, and spiritual well-being. Where most of my choices are made with the ability to consciously consider intentions of every action of everyone involved with the predictability of possibilities that always serve the right purpose.

#Story321: How do you find the truth?

By bypassing your ego and everything that your ego wants, needs, desires, fears. On the other side of all those walls is where you can access the truth.

#Story322: How do you and your wife solve your problems?

By directing our energy towards the problem, not towards each other. By viewing each problem as our enemy and not seeing each other as an enemy. That alone will help see clarity in each situation.

#Story323: Question: What do you mean by respect isn't real?

Answer: How is it real? Any subjective virtue will have a different meaning to seven-some billion people. Are you saying that you live your life based on respect, both giving and receiving? That's a lot of guessing. Love, on the other hand, is universal and it overwrites every virtue. See it as the master key that opens (and closes) all doors. Do you think that I need or expect respect from you or anyone else who's reading this? What good would it serve and why would I value it? How would my life be different if you showed me respect for the words I'm writing? So how can it be real? How can respect be real?

#Story324: Where do you see yourself in 5 years?

I try to stay away from daydreaming as much as possible. Envisioning myself years from now would be me trying to escape my reality here and now. With that said, I still like to play with the predictability of my life based on choices and somewhat constant variables. I like to see myself as someone who can contribute to the wellbeing of our society.

#Story325: Intuition or fact?

Whichever takes you where you need to be. Don't overthink it. If you overthink it, intuition's power is being taken away and you're letting your mind decide. Your intuition is there to cover you when your mind is overwhelmed.

#Story326: Everything you feel.

Everything you feel is real, but not eternal. Know that there is another world on the other side of your pain. Don't unpack and live in your current emotional state. Don't limit yourself to states when there is a whole universe that you can access.

#Story327: Anger towards police.

It's not the police that you resent. It's your disobedience in you that is trying to fight the obedience. It's just internal and your feelings towards uniformed law enforcement comes from the within. Their job serves you as well. They are human just like you. Don't judge them based on what they do, just like you don't like to be judged for what you do.

#Story328: Mental health stigma.

Mental illness is invisible. It doesn't have a face, color, race, or religion. It's hidden and rooted. It's every day, normalized symptoms. They are covered with facades and sometimes with smiles. They also show up as isolation, canceled plans, outbursts, meltdowns, feeling of burden, and persistent anxiety. It can be your friend, colleague, your neighbor, your parents, your children. It can be You. It's most often stigmatized by those who belong to it. It's about time we start realizing that everything is about mental health. We have run away from it for way too long.

#Story329: What inspired you to start Eigengro?

I realized that there was a need for life guidance through a sophisticated spiritual, mental and philosophical self-awareness approach based on the concept of natural law. Eigengro is not about giving people advice on how to live, but rather, is the mirror of who they are so they can find all the answers they need to continue their life-journey in a happier, more fulfilled, content, enlightened, and abundant way.

Eigengro teaching is based on my belief of a concept of self, governed not by exterospectional social forces nor by introspection beliefs, but rather, ones elevated mental and spiritual ability through observation of all things external, reflecting and evaluating all things internal to examine one's spiritual, emotional and mental state.

#Story330: The path of Eigengro.

When you close your eyes, why does the world in front of you disappear? Because your eyes are blocking out light and because you perceive the world with your sight. There is another world that most people don't see and that they are not aware of. That's where our awareness comes from. Our awareness doesn't originate from the external world but from our inner world.

The less balanced we are, the less access we have to our inner world. The less access to our inner world, the more we have the tendency to rely and operate, and run on programs and social norms without awareness that there is more than what we perceive with our senses. The world that you see when you open your eyes is created from the world that you don't see. Eigengro is one's own personal path and framework where we experience ourselves, our existence, the essence of ourselves, our purpose, role in society, and spiritual connection to nature and everything else around us.

My inspiration for the name Eigengro comes from German word Eigengrau which is the gray color seen in complete darkness. It is called brain gray. In complete darkness, the brain creates the perception of seeing a uniform dark gray. This is due to the optic nerve firing even without light. The color Eigengrau is *lighter* than black, even in the absence of light, than something black in normal light.   This is because in normal light, the contrast that light creates with the black makes the black appear darker. The Eigengro allegory is that even in complete darkness in life, there still is light and hope. I'd like to bring more awareness to light that we are not aware of and that we have access to, but our everyday life and routines have blocked us from accessing that light and awareness. I want this world to be brighter, more peaceful, and live in more harmony and balance. I know that it can be accomplished.

#Story331: Question: Why do I attract a certain type of people?

Answer: It's not about attraction. It's about you recognizing the same type of energy that you carry. You automatically get grouped together with other people who are similar to the phase you are in. It's difficult to grow if you surround yourself with people who are similar and who will always comfort you by telling you that you're a badass and the rest of the world is against you.

#Story332: The Holy System.

See it as a family or a guardian, but without a soul. You can get basic protection, knowledge, faith, information, communication, and charity. The system is constructed projection of our inner world. It's a matrix. It has no actual soul, but it's the manifestation of the soul that has been structured based on the accumulation of external needs, rules, beliefs, knowledge, and imbalances that reflect our inner needs, beliefs, and imbalances. The system is the projection of who we are and who we have become. It's a giant wheel and it continues going forward. You can't destroy it. The system can only be mastered. The system only changes if we change ourselves on the inside. You master it by mastering yourself. You can be a part of, you can exit it, you can fly above it, under it, through it. You can become one with it, sometimes you even decide to go against it. You can do anything you want and the system will have no problem with it as long as you don't interfere with its patterns of operation. It has no ability to give you individual attention. You can be at peace with it once you are at peace with yourself.

#Story333: The system can't hear you.

Why are you mad at the system? You can scream all you want, but the system doesn't hear you. Emotions and anger come from our inner wounds, triggered by what we see in the outside world (the system) when we subconsciously recognize something that relates to our childhood and if we feel mistreated. It's always related to authority and some governing body that resembles our childhood when we were "forced" to obey and follow the rules.

As adults, we are once again forced to follow the rules and those rules come from the same programs, but this time around it's not our parents or guardians but the system. We recognize it subconsciously and we get emotional; sometimes mad and angry at it. When those emotions resurface, regardless if it's empathy, anger, joy, or need for belonging, we react strongly. Not just us, others do too, and that's how we start grouping ourselves and start belonging or fighting for a cause. It feels good to channel it all out. It makes us believe and feel that there is a change happening now. And sometimes there is a change, but sometimes the change needs to happen on the inside in order for us to recognize what outside change is truly needed and what is just our personal projection. Personal projections make us vulnerable for agendas and falling into the trap of those behind them.

#Story334: You run the system. It doesn't run you.

The system is not multidimensional, it can only see what you present on the surface. It has no way and no ability to penetrate to the core of it all where the source of yours, mine and the systems energy comes from. That's where everything is decided, where all the major changes and growth is happening. What we see on the surface and within the construct is just the final cut of all the raw content that is being created within ourselves. You can learn how to become a creator of that content that the system uses. You feed into the system. You don't let the system feed into you. In order for you to accomplish that, you must be in charge and in control of yourself. It's a matter of personal growth where you are at peace with your triggers, emotions, and your mind. It's a level where you are safe from possible energy pulls that come from external forces. When you grow, heal, and master yourself, you will run the system, instead of it running you. Yes my friend, it only takes one individual to tame the system. If you think about it, the system is only one individual. It can be you.

#Story335: The Masters.

Masters make the rules. I've identified seven master programs and dozens of sub-programs that we all belong to. It's not bad. They actually help us get things straightened out. The goal is to recognize the good and the bad in the masters. The only way to master the masters is by being the master of yourself. That's the only way to be able to see things for what they are. All master programs start as rebellion programs and transition into master programs. Currently there is one main rebellion (disobedience) program that is active.

The Masters (Obedience) are:
1. Religion (Spirituality)
2. Nuclear Family
3. Authority (Obedience)
4. Republica (Society)
5. Imperia (Patriotism)
6. Academia (Knowledge, Indoctrination)
7. Media

The Rebellion Program:
1. Social Media/Internet (Disobedience)

It's up to you to interpret the above programs. Throughout my 369 stories you'll find all eight programs constantly present with or without your awareness. You'll see good and you'll see bad in them. It all depends on how much healing you have to do. The more healing, the more bad will you be able to see in each program.

Love is the only energy that is able to bypass all the guards of all master programs and access divine wisdom. There is no other energy that is able to bypass the doors of each guard that protect the programs. Love rules the world. Love is the most profound wisdom there is.

"Love rules the world.
Love is the most profound
wisdom there is."

#Story336: Who are we? Why are we?

It's genetically embedded in us to ask those questions. The curiosity of human existence and its timeline has captured the attention of philosophers, scientists, and individuals throughout history. Some people settle for what they know and some are seekers who continue the curiosity journey trying to solve the enigma of who we are and what we are doing on Earth. Also, who were the first living creatures to inhabit our planet?

Answers that we have discovered throughout history have led to consolidation and structured belief systems such as Religion, Science, and Philosophy. Do you need to know more than what you know? No, you don't, if what you know gives you peace and balance. If you are content where you are, there is no reason to search for something else.

#Story337: PHILOSOPHY, SCIENCE, RELIGION, CONSPIRACY.

They all come from our search to understand life and our existence. If we free ourselves from limitations of totalitarian dogmas of organizational spiritual belief system and agenda driven scientific research, we'll be able to recognize the value of information and truth in both science and religion if we focus on the purity of the message. Science calls for facts, and religion calls for faith, but where do we draw the line as far what is what?

Science uses hypothesis, experiments, and patterns to accomplish an understanding of physical reality. Science provides us with a greater insight into external physical reality than any rival systems of knowledge. Scientific evidence indicates that human existence is much older than what religion suggests. It states that the modern humans are 200,000 years old, but we still can't find much evidence further back than 6,000-8,000 years. This makes both science and religion right. We have been around for a while, but this latest version of us (civilization) is not older than 6,000-8,000 years, just as Religion suggests.

But why can't they both be right? If we stop and think about it, we need to separate the spiritual and the physical evolution. It is evident that we are not the first civilization on Earth. Both science and religion can agree.

Between science and religion, there is philosophy, which exists on different levels and with different
approaches that balances and evaluates science and religion while it attempts to understand the nature of man, existence, and the relationship that exists between the two concepts.

Conspiracy theorists, on the other hand, believe that an alien race that came here to escape their dying planet. They set up their civilizations and seeded the Earth.

The truth is, many things on this planet can't be explained by our current understanding of our existence. For example throughout the world, ancient cities are being discovered under the ocean with structures that display a level of technology scientists say was not possible at the time. But if those structures existed, then it must have been possible? What are these ancient underwater cities? Are they evidence of a pre flood civilization?

#Story338: The journey continues.

We continue to live, love, create, and explore as we keep our minds open and keep searching for the truth. We don't search for the truth so we can prove others wrong, or tell others what to do and how to live. We search for the truth so we can live a happier, more peaceful, and balanced life. Regardless of our belief systems and discoveries, it all becomes useless if it doesn't give us a sense of peace and harmony. Nothing in this world that has been accomplished without love, understanding and fulfillment is not worth accomplishing or searching for.

#Story339: When deciding to help others.

I always ask myself the following questions before making a decision to help:

- Will it take anything away from my close family and people that are my priority?
- Is help provided on an individual or collective level? If for an individual, did the person reach out directly or did you take the step to offer and why?
- What is the cause of the problem that I'm trying to solve by helping and will my involvement feed into the problem even more?
- How do I know that it helps? Does it only help myself by making me feel that I'm making a difference or does it truly help change the course of humanity?
- Can I track the progress until the very end and, if yes, how?
- Will my help and involvement cause any negative effects?

It's much better to live a life where everything you do is somehow affecting people positively every single day with every action you take. To me, THAT'S how we make a change that truly matters.

#Story340: What/Who is ERAHANT?

ERAHANT is the highest level of Enlightenment that I've discovered in my search for the truth. A person who is able to recognize and acknowledge everyone else's truth while staying true to his or her own truth. Having the ability to be ONE with everything while not belonging to anything. A master of it all. A new breed of a human who's guided by light to guide others to their own light. Erahant is someone who lives his life where everything becomes a choice and not a necessity.

"Eigengro is the path.
Erahant is the destination."

#Story341: Supporting Politicians.

I don't even support my own decisions and actions all the time, so why would anyone choose sides when it comes to politics and people who are associated with it? I can approve or disapprove policies, ideas, or values that politicians stand behind, but I don't know any of them on a personal level in order to fully support their actions. It's a career like anything else and they are all people with their own insecurities, struggles, demons, qualities and just like all of us they too search for answers and to heal themselves. I look at their passions, it tells me a lot about their intentions.

#Story342: Question: Who was/is your mentor?

You can learn something new from every single person that you meet in your life if you're open to receiving new information. I've had a lot of people who have influenced my life at different stages, but I have been my own shepherd most of my life. I've learned the most from ordinary everyday interactions with different people.

#Story343: I believe in miracles.

I was a man who was challenged to make some of the hardest decisions in my life at my weakest moments while believing that I was at my strongest. The moment when I could have had everything and nothing at the same time, depending on choices I made and the next steps I took. This was the time when darkness and pain slowly transitioned into brightness and happiness. The time when I could finally start seeing clarity and hope again without fully understanding how. The time when I started believing in miracles.

Who I'm today is the outcome of my still evolving journey. I want people to believe in their own journey like I believe in mine. This is my way of showing you who reach out to me that your life is important and that some things and events in your life that may appear a certain way could be something else and that there is a reason to what you're going through some hardship. No matter how your life currently is, or what you may be going through, your life, and your journey are equally important as anyone else's in this world regardless of their level of "success."

"Once you achieve a state of happiness you will no longer look for ways to define it."

#Story344: Question: How can I make my man happy?

Answer: Do not put so much responsibility on yourself when it comes to your man's happiness. That is something that only he can find within himself and with your help. Here are some of the things you can do that will be of value and help for him:

- Let him be a man as long as he understands what it means to him.
- When he acts out and is angry is when you have the biggest chance to make a positive change and impact on him by understanding that those emotions are manifestation of things that have happened to him.
- Observe, listen, analyze and show affection. Don't argue as that is exactly what he doesn't need as you will push him further away from you. Instead, bring up those things that he said and that hurt you only later when he is calm and when he will be open to receive the message.
- Be gentle and loving, but not a pushover. You need to set boundaries in order to gain his respect for you.

#Story345: Am I too ugly to be loved?

Soul and heart have no face nor body. Only those who don't have the ability to love others are ugly. Stop looking outside for answers and for love. Search deeper within yourself and define who you are based on truth, and not based on your or someone else's perception of your beauty. Once you start discovering yourself, you will start coming out of your shell and be able to connect with people based on who you are and not based on what you look like.

#Story346: How did you keep all the haters out when working towards your goals?

By shutting down the passage that helps them get to me. Once I found a way to close that door, I became an abstract thought for them. For each trigger you locate and dissolve, the less haters you will notice.

#Story347: Why is it so hard to find a lasting relationship after 40?

Because your focus is on making it last instead on focusing on the actual relationship. If people you date feel that you're sending a vibe that you want to trap them into something so you can secure your agenda, they will all run away. Focus on people and on the here and now, not on making something lasting. If you do things right here and now, there is no need to fear the future.

#Story348: Meeting toxic people.

When people say that they always meet toxic people that bring them down, they are just meeting the same people in different bodies. In order for you to recognize the quality in people you need to be able to appreciate, value, and experience the joy and gratitude of solitude. That's when you locate your own qualities that help you define who you truly are and who you are not. Suddenly you may experience an immense change in people you attract and who can further your growth.

#Story349: Thoughts on open relationships?

I like to keep my mind open, not my relationship. When you open your relationship you also open yourself and your partner for everything bad that other people can bring into your lives. Maybe it works for others, but I'm sure they have a way of dealing with all the side effects of such an arrangement. Also, what is that other people can give you that your partner can't? Maybe it's ourselves we need to start working on so we minimize the need of external stimulation. Anything we do based on pleasure and physical needs with multiple people may create emotional dark tunnels with ourselves and some of them can be hard to get out of.

#Story350: What is the most attractive quality in a woman?

A woman who takes the time to understand a man and where he comes from during his lowest moments in life. Being by his side through those time elevates her attractiveness by light years. It establishes a connection that goes beyond the physical attraction. That's a quality that will win every man's heart, no doubt.

#Story351: How do you determine whether someone likes/loves you?

Focus on loving them instead. That's easier to determine. (Romantic) Love should be as unconditional as possible. If they don't love you, their actions will show. You don't need to play a guessing game.

"Avoid trying to help someone fix their problems
until you solve your own problems. You will not
be helping. You will be projecting. That can lead
to an emotional havoc for both yourself and
others."

#Story352: What is the meaning of *smart*?

We can't measure something that has no limitations. There are measurable objectives and learning patterns around social constructs that label people as smart and not smart. That's just programs that can't objectively measure the capacity of the human mind and what it can accomplish and when. By labeling, we set limits on ourselves.

#Story353: Christ Consciousness.

Christ Consciousness, also called Higher Consciousness, is the state of awareness of our true nature. It's the consciousness of a higher Self. It is a frequency of human consciousness that is capable of transcending animal instincts. The Godly power of transcendental reality that is beyond all physical laws and lower energies. It is the highest state of intellectual, emotional, spiritual maturity and balance that can be accomplished through personal growth and righteousness through the path of love in life.

"Our peace is protected by finding the peace within us."

#Story354: Expanding horizons.

I believe that one may never allow himself to reach a philosophically progressional culmination during their lifetime. When we stop asking, searching, or questioning anything but rather choose to rely on recycled thoughts, ideas, citations, and references, we don't let the light pass through. We settle in life. Once we limit our intellectual and spiritual ability to expand its horizons, we will no longer be humans, but rather Artificial Intelligence.

#Story355: Catching yourself.

If you ever catch yourself being judgmental or blaming an isolated group of people, race, religion, status, color, age, or gender for any of your own problems, social problems or world problems, be very careful. This doesn't come from the truth, but from your wounds, triggers, programs, or media. No matter how right it feels to have those feelings, no matter what the history books, your parents or your friends tell you, this is nothing else but a personal issue that is a huge anchor for you. You will only get to grow and see the real truth once you take a step back and locate the cause of this projection. That is a big leak for darkness to come in and steer you towards all destinations and agendas that will put you in trouble. If you can overcome this one, you will become a new person with completely different energy.

#Story356: Question: Do you ever stop being a parent?

Answer: No. We just need to know when to step away and let our children find their own way while we always stick around, observe, guide, listen, and support.

#Story357: Question: Is it true that the Devil can control you?

Yes, absolutely. But first it's important to understand or rather, to unlearn the meaning and the misconceptions behind its personification as expressed in many religions, cultures, and societies. Devil, Satan, Lucifer, Prince of Darkness...The labels, names, and visual artistic presentations of the Devil are many. But it is the same hostile, negative, dark, and destructive force that is a part of the entire humanity - the same as the brightness, positivity, and the good force is also. We experience it both within us and around us daily. That road rage outburst, the co-worker argument, that friend's divorce, that sexual child abuser we saw on the news, that civil war in a third world country. It is all the same darkness that operates within different dimensions. The more imbalances we have within us, the more power "the Devil" will be able to gain and control. When the Devil completely takes over our entire being, we no longer have the ability to distinguish between good or bad and our ability to think, rationalize, feel, express ourselves is no longer controlled by our higher essence and our brightness. That also means that our actions seem justified and we start seeing the entire world as our enemy unless we recognize that very same dark energy. If that happens, we group ourselves

with it and we try to multiply it and spread it. The good thing is that the darkness or the devil is always self-destructive and that's why the brightness
always wins, but damages are always inevitable depending on the level of the Devil's ability to spread discord, as in the example I gave earlier with road rage or an argument. Always be observant and cautious of yourself. Only you have the power to tame the Devil. If it comes to the point that an outside force such as the law has to interfere, then you have lost your grip of it!

#Story358: Speak.

They'll tell you to listen instead of speaking, but I would like to tell you to not be afraid to speak. When you speak, if you speak from a place of purity and good intentions, you may discover knowledge and wisdom that you previously didn't have access to. Speaking many times acts as a catalyst to tap into higher dimensions. If you only listen with your ego, you still don't learn anything. It's all about how you listen, how you speak, and what your intentions are.

"Nostalgia is a liar trying to fool you by telling you that it was better before. Stay here and be now."
"It's not that many great people are wrong. It's just that they are half right."

#Story359: Still a warrior.

It's okay to be compassionate and kind but when someone invades your territory and threatens your well-being or your family's well-being, don't be afraid to become a warrior and protect yourself. It's not always a physical fight. Many times it's bad vibes or a pull from different (dark or negative) sides that comes from people around us on a daily basis. Fight it away.

#Story360: How to monitor yourself?

By fixing one personal issue at the time, starting with your biggest problems. As you grow, so will your awareness. Once your awareness starts getting a grip of your ego, it will start challenging it. It will hold you accountable before other people even notice it. When that happens, you start filling yourself with light, truth, and fulfillment.

#Story361: What do I want?

I truly try not to be pushy with my opinions and thinking. I want to be the last person to tell you what to do. Everyone else is already doing it. I want you to find your own answers and I hope to help you remove some of that pressure and pain you carry around while still sleep-walking through life. I don't want you to give up looking for meaning and purpose and I don't want you to stop asking important questions. It's okay if you don't find all the answers. You have your entire life ahead of you.

#Story362: Confession.

During a very intense phase of my journey as I started discovering more, my growing awareness showed me that I was projecting my personal issues with what I was pointing out and sharing with the world. However, many were still agreeing with me as so many shared the same issues and views and it was a great feeling that validation. I also started realizing that I wasn't providing any proper solutions, but I was instead, ranting about all our issues on a very intense level. I immediately paused everything and realized I needed to turn this into my own journey first before I presented anything to anyone. That's the reason I never saved any highlighted stories, archived posts, and went back to correct many of them. I like to hold myself accountable and question everything I do and say before I can completely be sure that my help would truly be "help."

It has worked great because I realized that the darkness I saw at the time was not all darkness and that our world the way I see it today is actually much brighter and more beautiful than my initial discoveries were. Also, I've found more beauty in people than ever before. That alone has narrowed down the number of issues and helped me provide more concise solutions to those who may find it helpful. I'm almost there.

#Story363: Sacrifice is not really sacrifice.

A personal sacrifice that serves my family and brings me closer to them is never a sacrifice. It's a personal accomplishment, a won battle and a step closer to my truth. Seeing it as a sacrifice is just our mind playing tricks on us trying to create emotional layers of self-pity, martyrdom, and self-inflicted pain. Releasing myself from everything that stands in between my family and what's best for them is exactly how things are supposed to be. The rest will fall into place.

#Story364: You're always in charge of what you let in.

My point is, everything in this world has good and bad in it. Most of the time, we can be completely in charge what we allow in and what we don't. The society we have today and the construct that we have created is not all bad. It's there to serve a purpose. It's here for a reason. Let's all work with it, around it, through it...whatever helps, but it all starts with that change within ourselves. If we don't make that change, we will never know what we are signing up for because we won't be able to recognize the good in the bad and the bad in the good. If it's not the digital world, something else will replace it. Whatever it is, we can always be in charge of the outcome and the effect it has on us.

#Story365: Taming the animal within.

We operate in the outside world by reacting to aspects of our inner world and inner well being. The rebellion in us will eventually betray us and let us down if we don't have the right discipline to tame what needs to be tamed. There are only so many chances the outside world will give us. We can't always rely on reactions that come from our elemental essence of our lower animal nature. It's smart to set personal boundaries between ourselves and ourselves. The world can be cruel and unforgiving. Master it so you can master the world.

"Any knowledge that has ever been spoken out into this world will always be out there vibrating. It doesn't have to be written or documented. We can still access it if we tune into the right frequencies."

#Story366: Single, but not alone.

To all the single peeps out there, never let your broken heart be occupied by resentment and hate. Your soulmate will be looking for the good in you so always make sure your beauty shines through and never let it be trapped inside darkness that life tries to throw at you.

#Story367: From fear to wings.

Only when you are prepared to fully face the fear of losing everything and everyone that you once thought were important - letting all of it go to ashes - is the only time you'll realize that the same things, and people whose pressure and expectations once brought you down to your knees, are the same things and people that become your wings of elevation and growth. Once your fear is replaced with truth, you become an architect of your destiny.

"The fall of man is the rise of ego. Realization is
just the expansion of your higher self."

#Story368: Evolution.

Today, we are expected to believe and accept that fossilized remains of "Lucy," a discovery that could have been completely staged, should serve as the basis of our human origins. People who choose to believe in accuracies of such "evidence" are welcome to do so. Human evolution is not physical and can't be documented. It can only be experienced. If there was a way to document and present "evidence," our ego-driven, ancestrally flawed civilization would find a way to distort and profit from it. We got to eat from the Tree of Knowledge, but the Tree of Life (where our truth is) can only be accessed once we have purified and freed ourselves from ourselves. The latest version of humanity dates back about 8,000 years and we have no need to search further back as there is absolutely nothing there...

There is a difference between adaptations based on natural selection and evolution. Natural selection is a process whereby physical or behavioral traits allows organisms to survive better. That does occur. However, just because we have similarities between other animals like fish, other mammals and monkeys, that doesn't prove that we came from fish or monkeys.

Wouldn't it make sense that living creatures were made from the same building blocks? Many people define evolution, when it pertains to humans, to mean we evolved from lower animal forms. But human consciousness/soul is unique and has nothing to do with the physical changes and adaptability. Even if we got completely wiped off the Earth physically, our consciousness would be transferred to another physical shape (body), human shape or not. What makes us human and gives us a sense of existence is our ego that was given to us as a gift to be able to experience life that is perceived through our senses.

Animals and humans share many of the same DNA sequences. Meaning the same DNA pattern. Humans and monkeys share about 99 percent. We also share DNA with plants. That's why many scientists say we are apes or a type of ape. Or we evolved from other species. But that's like saying chairs and homes are made 99% of the same thing-wood, bolts etc., then homes evolved from chairs. Why would God start from scratch from each species? Just because there are shared components, DNA, etc. doesn't, doesn't mean that we necessarily evolved from other forms. So, that's what I mean by even though we have the same building blocks and are similar, it doesn't necessarily mean we evolved from other species.

Nothing in this world is a coincidence. Even you reading this book is no coincidence. Everything is organized and the way it's supposed to be. Chaos only exists in our head but even that chaos is balanced out and gets organized in the bigger picture (equation of our reality). As humans, we are limited by our own minds and our egos that make us believe we know truths about our world and our history. Only when we can understand there is more, are we able to consider past that.

#Story369: Your story starts here.

This is where your #Story1: begins. Write your 369 stories. It took me 12 months to write mine. Take the time you need to write yours. I hope to read them at some point. Share them with me and others on Eigengro.com.

"I can only help those who still search for answers, not those who believe that they have already found them."

60963434R00245

Made in the USA
Middletown, DE
16 August 2019